Cost Analysis in Education

EDI Series in Economic Development

Cost Analysis in Education

A Tool for Policy and Planning

Philip H. Coombs and Jacques Hallak

Published for The World Bank
The Johns Hopkins University Press
Baltimore and London

Library of Congress Cataloging-in-Publication Data

Coombs, Philip Hall, 1915-
    Cost analysis in education : a tool for policy and planning /
Philip H. Coombs and Jacques Hallak.
      p.   cm. -- (EDI series in economic development)
    Bibliography: p.
    ISBN 0-8018-3648-4 (Johns Hopkins University Press)
    1. Education--Costs--Accounting. 2. Educational planning.
I. Hallak, Jacques. II. Title. III. Series.
LB2830.C66 1987
338.4'337--dc19
                                                        87-26105
                                                        CIP

Foreword

In 1972, UNESCO's International Institute of Educational Planning (IIEP) published *Managing Educational Costs*, by Philip H. Coombs and Jacques Hallak, based in part upon a number of cost analyses that IIEP had sponsored in developing countries. The book was one of the first to deal with the subject of cost analysis in the education sector and was well received.

With the passage of time, that book and the cases on which it was based became increasingly out of date. By the early 1980s, it was out of print. Yet some portions of the book made very useful background readings in seminars on educational finance and management held at the Economic Development Institute (EDI) of the World Bank. We thought it would be useful—not only for EDI, but also for other institutions that provide training for education sector managers around the world—to have portions of the book revised so it could be available once again.

The original authors agreed to undertake a substantial revision, adding insights from their experience in the intervening years and developments in cost analysis methodology since the early 1970s. UNESCO, the International Institute of Educational Planning, and the Oxford University Press kindly granted EDI permission to publish a shortened, updated, and modified version. The World Bank and EDI are grateful to these institutions for the rights to use portions of the earlier work.

In a surprising number of instances, ministries of education in developing countries do not have good data on unit costs of the main types and levels of education that would enable managers to improve efficiency and effectiveness. The present volume is intended to inform educational managers, who do not routinely have access to cost data for planning and other management tasks, about why it is important to have adequate information on the costs of education, what kinds of information they should have, how such information may be used to improve management and efficiency, and how to go about collecting the information. It is not a technical manual on cost analysis methodology. It provides instead a general orientation toward gathering and using cost data to guide decisions. An important aspect of the book is the *philosophy* of cost analysis it embodies: a practical, down-to-earth approach to the task of measuring and estimating educational costs, and then using the information to ensure that the education system makes the best use possible of its scarce resources. Because it is often not possible to obtain highly precise cost data, the authors make it clear that according to their philosophy it is permissible—indeed even preferable—to settle for *reasonably* accurate indicators that can be prepared quickly and at low cost.

One category of readers will be participants in seminars and courses on education management, planning, and finance offered at the EDI and at other training institutions throughout the world. But we hope that other readers will find the book interesting and useful, especially working education managers at all levels in education systems in developing countries. If they can gain a sense of using information to guide decisions, knowing how much things cost (including such concepts as "opportunity cost"), and using scarce resources to produce the most learning possible, then the book will have achieved its purpose.

R. W. McMeekin
Education and Training Design Division
Economic Development Institute
June 1987

Contents

Preface

This book is about the economics of education, but it is written mainly for noneconomists. It is intended for people who actually run formal education systems or nonformal education programs and who practice planning, decision making, and management every day or who are in training for such roles. These people include not only the handful of experts and officials in capital cities who make overall plans and top policies; they include all the people who work where the real action is—at the state, district, or community level—in individual schools, colleges, and universities, or in agricultural extension services, in skill training programs, or in any other type of nonformal educational activity.

All these people share responsibility for solving today's most crucial problem in education: how to provide better quality and more relevant education for an increasing number of learners with the limited resources available. This has always been a challenge to educational managers, but it is a far greater one today than ever before because of the formidable financial problems and related critical issues that have recently overtaken educational systems worldwide.

The basic thesis of this book is that cost analysis—of a more extensive and exacting kind than has generally been practiced in the past—is a powerful and indispensable tool for helping policymakers, planners, and educational practitioners at every level and in every country to cope more effectively. Thus the book's purpose is to dispel the mystique that so often surrounds cost analysis, and to provide a down to earth explanation of cost analysis that will enable its use by educational practitioners in their particular situations.

The book focuses on developing countries because they are most severely affected by the critical issues referred to above; however, the basic concepts and methods of cost analysis are equally relevant to the more developed nations. They too face serious educational problems today, including financial problems, and many of them are unsophisticated in their application of cost analysis.

This book is the sequel to our earlier book, *Managing Education Costs*, that was based on an extensive series of country case studies on cost analysis conducted by UNESCO's International Institute for Educational Planning (IIEP) in Paris in the late 1960s and early 1970s. Many people found that first book useful; however, one of its perennial users, the World Bank's Economic Development Institute (EDI), which conducts many training courses for development officials and experts from developing countries, recently suggested that a new, up to date version of the earlier book that took into account the great changes that have occurred on the world educational scene since the original book was published, would be helpful. The result is this book.

We take this opportunity to express our appreciation to the World Bank, and particularly to EDI staff, for their encouragement and help. We hasten to add, however, that we enjoyed full independence in writing the book and that we accept full and sole responsibility for its content. The views and interpretations expressed in these pages reflect our own experience and perceptions, and may or may not coincide with views held by various World Bank officials and specialists. We want also to thank UNESCO and the IIEP for making available useful illustrative materials, but again, these organizations bear no responsibility for how we have used their materials. Finally, our thanks also go to Frances O'Dell for her yeoman service in producing a legible manuscript, and to the Trustees of the International Council for Educational Development for their encouragement and cooperation.

Bear in mind that this book is essentially an introductory primer on educational cost analysis and on its counterpart, revenue analysis. It makes no claim to having the last word on the subject, for educational cost analysis is a dynamic field where new concepts and techniques are constantly being devised, debated, and tested. Those who wish to dig more deeply into the subject or to find further examples of the many different ways in which countries have applied cost analysis should refer to the selected reading list at the end of the book, and to the much more extensive bibliographies contained in some of those references.

Philip Coombs and Jacques Hallak

1. The Setting

The world educational crisis that erupted in the 1970s has profoundly altered the financial posture of educational systems everywhere (see Coombs 1985, especially Chapter 5). During the halcyon years of the 1950s and 1960s, when education budgets in virtually all countries were expanding rapidly, the big question facing policymakers and educational managers was how best to allocate the sizeable annual increments among different educational levels and uses. Today, however, with most countries' educational budgets frozen or shrinking, the daunting question is where to make the cuts?

This adverse financial situation is tied to several other critical educational issues that are currently plaguing both developing and developed nations (though in different degrees of intensity). They include (1) the erosion of educational quality and relevance and the often dubious contribution of education to individual and national development; (2) the increasing numbers of "educated unemployed" and the growing incongruities between the world of education and the world of work; (3) the gross educational inequalities that penalize females, the poor, and various ethnic minority groups; (4) the declining status and attractiveness of teaching as a profession; (5) the deterioration of international educational cooperation; and (6) most worrisome of all, the waning public confidence in education.

Even the richest industrialized nations are having to face these critical problems, but by far the most serious victims are the low-income developing nations, especially in Africa. The latter have a quintuple disadvantage: slim and overstrained resources; relatively low school participation rates and literacy rates; imported educational models that are often ill-suited to the countries' circumstances; saturated employment markets; and high population growth rates that generate continuing powerful pressures to expand enrollments.

In the face of adverse financial circumstances, the central challenge to educational managers everywhere is to find ways to use their limited resources more efficiently and effectively and to augment these resources by tapping new sources of revenue.

How Cost Analysis Can Help

Cost analysis is a versatile and potentially powerful tool to meet the above challenge, but education managers should not think of it as a panacea. Indeed, no simple remedies exist for overcoming the problems they face. To cope with them effectively will require a combination of bold, inventive,

1

and persistent measures involving far-reaching changes in traditional educational forms and practices, as well as sizeable changes in the economic, social, and political environment surrounding education.

What cost analysis can do is to help educational managers see the various options and trade-offs available to them more clearly, and assess their relative merits and feasibility. It can reveal the possible advantages of redeploying limited resources between different levels and types of education, between different categories of inputs, and between different geographic areas. Cost analysis can uncover serious internal waste and inefficiency and possible ways to eliminate them. It can also suggest ways to enhance the external productivity of education and the benefits accruing to individuals and society from well-directed investments in education.

In addition, cost analysis is an essential tool for testing the economic feasibility of broad national education plans, of specific project plans, and of proposed innovations. By so doing, it can help policymakers to seize important opportunities, and to avoid heading off in superficially attractive directions that turn out to be deadends.

To accomplish such useful purposes, however, cost analysis must usually be combined with different types of pedagogical analysis designed to assess the learning outcomes of any educational process. The key to judging the efficacy of an educational process lies in comparing the costs invested in it and the learning results attained.

Cost analysis must also be combined with revenue analysis, because the amount of revenue available for any given period fixes the outer limits of possible expenditures. Any educational plan that ignores these limits is heading for trouble.

We wish to emphasize here our earlier point, that the various uses of cost analysis, as well as the basic cost concepts and principles discussed later, are equally applicable to both formal and nonformal education. In practice, however, practitioners must allow for the wide differences between various nonformal educational activities: in their organization, objectives, and types of clienteles served; in their sources of support and types of inputs required; and in their teaching and learning arrangements. Most of the examples used in this book are drawn from formal education systems, but those familiar with nonformal education should be able to think of comparable nonformal examples.

What Makes a Good Cost Analyst

Good educational cost analysts can literally be worth their weight in gold—provided they ask the right questions and arrive at responsible answers, and provided the decisionmakers understand the answers clearly and take them seriously.

To be a good educational cost analyst does not require a doctorate in economics or anything else. What it does require is an interest in education, a critical and inquiring mind, and an abundance of common sense. It also requires some fundamental statistical and analytical skills, a familiarity with basic cost concepts and how to apply them, and an intuitive impulse to view any educational system or subsystem as a system. Finally, it requires an ability to work well with others, and to work hard, imaginatively, and patiently in the face of incomplete and often imperfect data.

To these basic qualifications we add two important cautions. First, cost analysts should avoid becoming so totally enamored by and preoccupied with statistics, and with measuring the quantitative dimensions and relationships in any educational situation, that they ignore or dismiss the vital qualitative aspects of education, which cannot be measured. Some highly trained, quantitatively-minded economists and other social scientists tend to consider any factor they cannot measure statistically as unimportant or even unreal, whereas the unmeasurable factors are sometimes the most important of all. This is where observation, common sense, and wise judgment based on experience play a critical role.

Second, cost analysts must be aware of the danger inherent in designing an ingenious model or scheme aimed at increasing the internal efficiency or external productivity of an educational system, without taking the trouble to examine whether it can actually be implemented, not just financially, but administratively and politically. Many attractive theoretical models have come to grief because their designers failed to consider the practical requirements and constraints involved in putting them into action.

Using the Past to Foresee the Future

Educational costs analysts and planners constantly have to visualize the future. They can do this more realistically if they understand the past well; the policies, assumptions, and motivations, and the economic, social, and political forces that have shaped their country's present educational situation.

History will probably not repeat itself, nor will past trends follow a straight-line path into the future. However, observable forces in action today grew out of the past and are already shaping education's future. Thus, the cost analysts and planners who keep close watch on these forces are in a better position to anticipate their future movements and the kinds of impacts they are likely to have on educational costs and revenues. Obviously, no one can predict the future accurately; unforeseeable developments and surprises are bound to occur, but this does not mean that we must move into the future blindfolded.

A number of examples exist of past trends and developments that foreshadowed and contributed to the critical educational issues currently facing both developing and developed countries. As we look back over the past few decades, three particularly striking phenomena stand out. The first is the dramatic quantitative expansion of educational systems worldwide. Between 1960 and 1980, according to UNESCO estimates, total world enrollments (at all levels combined) roughly doubled, rising from 327 million to 641 million. In other words, world enrollments increased as much in a single generation as in all previous history. This was indeed an impressive achievement, even allowing for the fact that these statistics are somewhat inflated, especially for developing countries.

The second, very encouraging, phenomenon is that the bulk of this great expansion was achieved by the developing countries, which boosted their

3

share of the world total from 45 percent in 1960 to 63 percent in 1980.[1]

The third phenomenon, especially germane to this book, is that total world public expenditures on formal education increased more than ten-fold during 1960 to 1980, from about US $50 billion in 1960 to nearly US $600 billion in 1980 (measured in current prices and converted to U.S. dollars). Thus, educational expenditures increased five times as much as enrollments, which means that over this period, the average expenditure per student increased about five-fold. Later we will examine why this happened. We will also show that part of this extraordinary increase in educational expenditures was eaten up by inflation, especially during the 1970s; but even so, a sizeable portion of it was "real."

A noteworthy point is that the division of total world expenditures on education between developed and developing countries has all along been extremely lopsided. In 1980, for example, the developed nations, with only 37 percent of total world enrollments, accounted for 88 percent of total public educational expenditures, whereas the developing nations, with 63 percent of total world enrollments, accounted for only 12 percent of total world expenditures. This partly explains why comparative studies of student achievement in mathematics and reading comprehension have shown much lower levels of achievement by primary and secondary students in developing countries than in the industrialized countries.

Yet ironically, the cost per pupil measured in terms of average per capita income, is generally higher in developing countries than in the richer developed countries, especially at the secondary and postsecondary level. This means that the citizens of developing countries—including many whose children never get to school or drop out early—are sacrificing more for education than the citizens of developed countries. It also means that developing countries can least afford to waste any scarce educational resources.

The global picture sketched above of the remarkable quantitative growth of education in recent decades tells only one side of the story—the bright side. We must also reckon with the dark side. For one thing, these composite figures conceal wide differences between individual countries and regions, and large disparities within individual countries between urban and rural areas, between different socioeconomic groups, and between the sexes. They also hide the brute fact that, despite the great increase in enrollments since 1960, at least half the children in many developing countries are still not getting a full primary education. Moreover, the number of out-of-school children and youth in the developing countries is greater today than 20 years ago, and is expected to increase further in the immediate future. The developing countries also have more illiterate adults today than they did 10 or 20 years ago, and this number is also expected to increase.

Most importantly, these indicators of education's impressive quantitative growth do not reveal what has been happening to the qualitative aspects.

---

[1] The above enrollment figures exclude China, for which data were not yet available. However, the figures on China published by UNESCO for the first time in 1983 make the above picture even more impressive. According to these new estimates, China's total enrollments as of 1980 were 204 million: equivalent to one-quarter of the world total and to one-third of the total for the developing countries.

They tell us nothing, for example, about what the students are being taught, how much they are actually learning, and how relevant and useful this learning is likely to be to their future lives and to the development of their society. These qualitative dimensions are admittedly far more difficult to determine than the number of students enrolled and the amount of money being spent on them. Nevertheless, strong indications exist that the quality and relevance of education has deteriorated seriously in a great many places, partly as a result of spreading limited resources over more students, and partly because the curricula and educational techniques and practices have not kept pace with the times. It follows that educational policymakers, planners, and managers should focus on improvement of these qualitative aspects.

Returning to expenditures, from the early 1950s to the early 1970s, public education budgets in most countries grew more rapidly each year—sometimes two to three times as rapidly—as the total public budget and the gross national product. Thus national education budgets received a steadily increasing percentage share of each nation's total expendable resources. This favorable priority was a great boon to educational expansion, as well as persuasive evidence of the great value that governments and their people attached to education. But this trend could obviously not continue indefinitely without seriously crippling other important public services and dislocating the whole economy. Thus by the mid-1970s, the rising trend of education's percentage share of national resources had flattened out in most countries, and in some it had begun to shrink. This was the beginning of the great budget squeeze that has plagued all educational systems ever since.

2. Education as a System

Before starting their work, cost analysts must have a clear and consistent understanding of educational costs and of the different types of costs, the forces that influence them, and the effects of those forces. Cost analysts must also understand the different types and sources of revenues needed to fuel educational costs and how such revenues behave under various circumstances. Chapters 2 and 3 will clarify these basic concepts and demonstrate the dynamic nature of educational costs and revenues.

To obtain a full and accurate picture of the reality they are concerned with, educational cost analysts must view an educational system *as* a system, that is, as a dynamic, organic whole composed of many interdependent parts (subsystems). They must also be constantly aware that any significant change in one part of the system, for example, a change in the proportions of its inputs or the intensity of their use, or a change in its technology, organization, or management, is likely to have substantial repercussions on other parts of the system, and almost certainly on its future costs and efficiency. By the same token, if any important component of the system is malfunctioning or missing, the performance of the system as a whole is bound to suffer.

It is for these reasons that a "systems analysis approach" is essential for educational cost analysis. By this we do not mean a sophisticated mathematical input-output model programmed for rapid calculation on a computer. Rather, we mean a conceptual analytical framework based on the same logical concepts as the mathematical model, but applicable even when some of the important variables (particularly the qualitative ones) are not susceptible to quantitative measurement. Note that for some purposes, however, a quantitative model can be useful, especially if reasonably good data are available; but a purely quantitative model cannot be expected to measure adequately the various important qualitative aspects of the system. (For a good example of a useful analytical model, see Zymelman and Yee 1985).

Before proceeding, we must distinguish between formal and nonformal education. Any nation's formal education system, viewed from bottom to top, is a true system in the strict technical sense, because all its various levels and parts constitute, at least in principle, an integrated whole. Referring to a nation's widely assorted nonformal educational activities as a nonformal education system is incorrect, however, because most of these activities have no direct operational relationship with each other. Individually, however, each activity can be correctly and usefully viewed as a system, either a separate system unto itself, such as a freestanding adult literacy program, or as an educational subsystem of a broader development program, such as an agricultural, health, or multipurpose community development program.

6

Five Key Elements of Any Educational System

Viewed through the lens of systems analysis, any educational system—formal or nonformal—has the following five cardinal features:

1. Objectives. The attainment of objectives is the system's reason for existing and its only warrant for commanding a share of scarce public and private resources. Most systems, especially formal education systems, have a variety of objectives, which are often in competition with one another; thus decisionmakers have to set priorities and mediate conflicts. The objectives range from very general and ambiguous goals for the system as a whole, such as producing good citizens, developing liberally educated leaders, and supporting national development, to more specific aims, such as mastering long division, fractions, and decimals, learning the basic principles of physics, developing elementary proficiency in a foreign language, or developing automobile repair skills.

Most nonformal education programs have more limited objectives that are tied to one or more immediate learning needs of a particular group. Most of the programs are part-time and of much shorter duration than formal schooling. Being inherently more flexible, nonformal education can adapt and respond more quickly to changing learning needs resulting from changing circumstances.

Sometimes an educational system's stated objectives differ considerably from its actual objectives as revealed by day to day activities. In a certain developing country, for example, an officially proclaimed goal of the school system may be to acquaint young people with their country's and region's history, culture, and geography, whereas in fact pupils spend an inordinate amount of time trying to master the language and learn about the history, culture, and geography of a distant metropolitan nation from which their country has gained independence. Another proclaimed aim may be to develop the capacity of young people to analyze problems rationally and to devise their own solutions, whereas in fact they spend most of their time memorizing other people's solutions.

If an educational system is not clear about its specific objectives and priorities, it lacks any rational basis and starting point for appraising and improving its performance, for planning its future, or for making good use of cost analysis for these purposes. Like a ship at sea without a compass, it has no clear notion of where it is going or how to get there.

2. Outputs. These include all the acquired learning, skills, insights, attitudes, styles of thinking—all the developed aptitudes and capabilities—that students carry away from the educational system beyond what they brought to it initially. In other words, the outputs are the "educational value-added" to the students by their exposure to the particular educational process.

The outputs cannot be adequately assessed simply by a standardized examination given to all students at the end of the process, especially if they entered the process with widely differing family and cultural backgrounds, career aspirations, motivations, and inherent abilities. Some students who do only fair to middling on the final examinations may well have gained more, relative to where they started from, than some who come out on top. Moreover, the key question is not simply how much the students learned, as revealed by final examinations, but how well their learning matched the system's objectives, and how well the objectives matched the real learning needs of the students and the society. Unless educational managers have a reasonably clear idea about these relationships, then all talk about the efficiency, quality, and productivity of the educational system is little more than empty rhetoric.

3. Benefits. The ultimate purpose of any educational system is not simply to produce immediate educational outputs and value-added in the sense just described, but to generate longer-term benefits accruing from the actual use of these immediate learning results.

The benefits take many forms, both economic and noneconomic, individual and social. Individuals, for example, may benefit by getting better jobs and higher lifetime earnings, by having more satisfying family lives, by adding richer cultural and civic dimensions to their existence, and by a greater sense of participation in the surrounding world. The society at large may benefit from higher production and better living standards, from an enlarged supply of effective leadership at every level, and from the enrichment of its culture through the release of greater creativity in more people.

If the society or the individuals were not reasonably confident of obtaining substantial benefits such as these, they would be foolish indeed to spend so much time, effort, and money on the educational system. What the benefits actually turn out to be, of course, depends not only on what the educational system produces, but also on how effectively the economy and society use these learning outputs.

In the case of formal schooling, such future benefits are often taken for granted, whether justifiably or not, but most nonformal education programs are put to a more rigorous test by their voluntary participants. If the participants conclude that what they are getting from the program is not worth the effort involved, they will simply stop coming. If enough people vote against it in this manner, the program will collapse. This explains, for example, the demise of so many rural adult literacy programs, especially in villages where participants have nothing available to read after they have made a major effort to learn how.

4. Internal Process. To produce useful outputs and longer-term benefits, an educational system must have effective ways of doing its work. It must have appropriate technologies and pedagogical methods, an effective organizational structure, logistical arrangements, and management provisions for orchestrating its many components. It must have appropriate means for judging and controlling the quality of its products and for assessing its own performance. It must also have a curriculum whose content is well related to the system's objectives and to the learner's needs. All these constitute the system's internal process.

Many people, including many educators, assume that the traditional form of education is the only available process, but many possible alternative processes exist, some better than others in terms of both costs and learning results. One important function of cost analysis is to help assess the relative merits and feasibility of these alternatives.

5. Inputs. These are the various resources and elements required to enable the system to function. They include not only students, teachers, and managers, but instructional materials, physical facilities, equipment, and supplies of various sorts. The amounts, quality, and proportions of various inputs needed depend not only on the number of learners to be served, but also on the nature of the particular system, of its objectives, and of the backgrounds and needs of the learners themselves. These inputs constitute the system's costs, whether they are expressed in physical ("real" resource) terms or in financial (monetary) terms.

Here again, nonformal education programs often differ considerably from each other and from formal education in their organization and internal process, in the combination of inputs used, and hence in their costs. Many of them have relatively low budgetary costs because they make extensive use of borrowed facilities, volunteer services, and other "nonmonetized" inputs that do not show up in their financial budgets. Nonformal education programs, however, do not automatically have low costs; some badly conceived ones have absurdly high costs.

Efficiency and Productivity

Having examined the five features of an educational system and the relationships between them, we can now define more precisely what is meant by an educational system's internal efficiency, its external productivity, and its cost-benefit (or benefit-cost) ratio—terms that are all too often used vaguely and ambiguously.

Internal Efficiency

Internal efficiency refers to the relationship between a system's (or subsystem's) outputs (learning achievements) and the corresponding inputs that went into creating them. Thus defined, an educational system's internal efficiency may be judged in terms of its cost-effectiveness, with effectiveness measured in this context by the system's immediate outputs as distinct from its ultimate benefits.[1] Any judgment of cost-effectiveness requires both an

---

[1] A frequently used but narrower concept of efficiency that is borrowed from engineering equates it with wastage, that is, dropout and repeater rates. Thus, for example, a primary school system is rated highly inefficient if half the pupils who enroll in Grade One drop out before completing Grade Six, and if in addition, the average "completer" repeats two grades along the way, taking eight years instead of six to finish the cycle. By this definition, a school system with no dropouts or repeaters would be 100 percent efficient (like a steam engine that converted 100 percent of the thermal energy of the coal it consumed into equivalent useful energy).

Wastage of this sort certainly contributes to inefficiency, but the problem with this concept is that it ignores other important forms of educational inefficiency that also reduce the system's cost-effectiveness. For example, a school system that has no dropouts or repeaters can still be inefficient if the learning results it produces over six years are very poor and not very relevant to the system's objectives and the learners' needs, or if the learning results—even if relevant and of good quality—could have been achieved at half the cost by some alternative method.

9

economic assessment to measure the cost of inputs, and a pedagogical assessment of the learning achieved. We use the term judgment advisedly because obtaining a precise measurement of learning achievements is seldom possible. Nevertheless, arriving at the best possible assessment of both the costs and the learning results is important, since their relationship is fundamental to evaluating the system's performance and comparing it with possible alternative educational approaches to the same learning objectives.

There are many ways to improve an educational system's internal efficiency, that is, to reduce its costs without a corresponding reduction in the learning results, or to improve the learning results without an equivalent increase in its costs. These improvements fall into three main categories according to the degree of change required in the present system.

1. Educational managers may improve efficiency by changing the amounts, quality, and proportions of inputs, or by using present inputs more intensively, without basically altering the system's existing structure and technology. Examples would be changing the pupil/teacher ratio or the mix of teachers' qualifications, enriching the instructional materials per pupil, or making greater use of buildings and equipment.

2. Going a step further, educational managers may increase efficiency by modifying the system's basic design by introducing distinctly new components and technologies, for example, team teaching, instructional radio or television, programmed self-instructional materials, or language laboratories.

3. A more radical approach to improving efficiency would be to design a new teaching-learning system that differs radically from the conventional one, for example, creating a distance learning system involving correspondence and radio, self-instructional materials, exercises, and simple do-it-yourself laboratory kits.

Of course not all changes or innovations will improve efficiency. Some may do quite the opposite. If 10 percent more inputs are added per student, for example, and their learning improves by only 3 percent, efficiency has actually declined because the costs have increased proportionately more than the learning results, worsening the cost-effectiveness ratio.

External Productivity

External productivity is related to internal efficiency, the main difference between them hinging on the distinction made earlier between immediate outputs and ultimate benefits. An educational system's external productivity is the relationship between the cost of producing learning results (outputs) in a particular period, and the cumulative benefits (individual and social, economic and noneconomic) that subsequently accrue from these learning results over a longer period. This same relationship is involved in assessing the system's (or subsystem's) cost-benefit ratio.

Paradoxically, an educational system can have high internal efficiency yet low external productivity. This happens, for example, when an educational system spends its time and resources efficiently teaching the wrong things—wrong, that is, in terms of its students' needs. An extreme example would be requiring Eskimo children to learn ancient Greek or tropical agriculture. The same happens when a system turns out far too many expensively trained specialists of certain types and too few of other types relative to the economy's manpower needs and employment opportunities. The first set of specialists may have been well trained, but if too few jobs are

10

available in that field, the investment in their training is likely to produce few benefits. The same resources devoted to training more of the specialists needed by the country would be far more productive.

Thus the relevance and fitness of what an educational system teaches its students at a particular time and place has a major bearing on the system's ultimate productivity. Of course there are also other determining factors that are external to the education system, such as the economy's ability to make efficient use of the supply of educated manpower, and the presence or absence of complementary forces of economic development. For example, well informed farmers are obviously essential for achieving a green revolution, but if the other essentials are missing, such as ample supplies of water, new varieties of seed, fertilizer, credit, and prices sufficient to cover farmers' costs and given them a reasonable profit, the educational efforts devoted to developing the necessary human resources for improved agricultural development may be largely wasted. In short, education is clearly a very important part of every development package, but it is still only a part. It cannot produce development by itself.

Cost-Benefit Ratios

An educational system's (or subsystem's) cost-benefit ratio is an important indicator of its external productivity. If the accrued benefits to individuals and to society substantially exceed the educational costs, then that particular educational effort can be viewed as a good investment.

Cost-benefit analysis can be used not only to assess the efficacy of past investments in education, but to assess the feasibility of a proposed future educational innovation, or the comparative merits of alternative educational approaches to the same learning objectives (see Levin 1983).

Cost-benefit analysis became a topic of interest and controversy, especially among economists, in the 1960s, when several ingenious economists (including Nobel Laureate Theodore Schultz, Edward Dennison, Gary Becker, and Mark Blaug) devised statistical methodologies for measuring education's contributions to national economic growth. Early studies had shown that the growth of an economy's output could not be fully explained simply by increased inputs of capital and labor; a sizable "residual factor" of growth needed to be explained. The economists' hypothesis was that the main ingredient of this residual factor was "educational investment in human capital," which increased people's productivity. They sought to prove this hypothesis by demonstrating that people with more years of education generally received higher wages and larger lifetime earnings, which reflected their higher productivity.

This line of reasoning led to the rate of return method of educational cost-benefit analysis, which has been tested in many countries. Interestingly, virtually all of rate of return studies concluded that (1) the economic rate of return on past investments in education has been significantly higher than in other fields of investment, such as industry; (2) the rate of return on elementary education has been substantially higher than on secondary and especially university education; and (3) the rate of return to individuals from higher education has been greater than the rate of return to society as a whole (due mainly to the heavy public subsidy of higher education).

The proponents of the studies claim that these statistical conclusions not only demonstrate the valuable contributions of education to economic growth in the past, but that they also provide useful guidance to policymak-

11

ers on where best to allocate investment funds in the future to maximize economic growth. (For a detailed explanation of the rate of return method see Psacharopoulos and Woodhall 1985).

Other economists, however, have criticized this rate of return approach on both practical and theoretical grounds. They point out, for example, that the data on educational costs and benefits, especially on wages and lifetime earnings, required for the calculations, are inadequate for reliable results. Moreover, they argue, simply to count the number of years of schooling each person has received ignores the issues of quality and relevance of their education. It also ignores three other important factors: the many out-of-school ways by which people acquire valuable learning; the significant noneconomic benefits that education can provide; and the many other factors, apart from education, that can influence the type of job and the level of income a person may get, such as personal motivation, family connections, and the condition of the economy and the employment market.

The most serious criticism, however, is that the rate of return figures—even if one were to accept them as being accurate—refer only to past conditions, and are not reliable predictors of future rates of return because of the dynamic changes taking place both in educational costs and output and in economic and employment conditions. In short, the critics assert, this may be an intellectually elegant methodology, fascinating to theoretically minded, neoclassical economists, but it is far too simplistic and too much like a statistical house of cards to provide trustworthy guides for future policy decisions.

You can make what you will out of this debate among economists, but whatever your conclusions, educational cost analysts should be acquainted with the methodologies, advantages, and limitations of the rate of return approach. Remember, before you accept the conclusions of any such study, you must examine closely how it was done, when it was done, and the adequacy of the educational cost and earnings data on which it was based. Remember too, as noted earlier, other methods and uses of economic analysis are available that can be useful for educational planning, evaluation, and decision making. A basic example is simple projection of the cost implications of policies, programs or projects, sometimes called "cost-feasibility analysis". This means multiplying a project's enrollment effects by estimated unit costs, which requires data on costs at the very least. Another tool is cost-effectiveness analysis, which means comparing alternative investment projects in terms of their relative *costs per unit of output*. Cost-effectiveness is a relative rather than an absolute measure. It is especially useful in the education sector, where outputs ("achievement", for example) do not have readily-observable, valid market prices. It is sometimes difficult to apply cost-effectiveness analysis because it is hard to identify and measure outputs. It is easy to compare costs per student year or per graudate of an educational cycle. Comparing the costs per unit of achievement, as measured on standardized tests, is much more problematical. Other indicators of educational outputs include rates of promotion to the next higher level of education, success in gaining employment (including indicators of time needed to find a job), and even subjective assessments of educational quality. Special studies are usually needed to generate such indicators of educational outputs, just as special studies are needed to measure school costs. Still such studies of educational outcomes are increasingly being conducted, including in developing countries, and they are very worthwhile. An absolute essential for any application of economics in education is to have good data on costs.

Almost any effort to measure statistically the internal efficiency, the external productivity, or the cost-benefit ratio of a formal or nonformal educational system is likely to be complicated and difficult. Pinning down all the inputs and costs correctly is hard enough, but identifying and quantifying all the significant learning results is much harder. Most difficult of all, however, is assessing the ultimate benefits, for these can take many different forms, and generally they cannot be attributed solely to an individual's formal schooling.

The value of the concepts just discussed is not diminished because they cannot be applied with caliper precision. They can be useful even in situations that defy all quantitative measurement. They are simply intelligent ways to approach any educational situation, ways that force analysts to ask the right questions and to examine the most critical relationships before reaching a final decision. Indeed, when an educational activity cannot be measured precisely, there is all the more need to approach it with a systematic method of analysis that will focus attention upon and invite careful judgments about the critical issues and relationships.

Different Ways to Express Educational Costs

Educational costs alone have little meaning. It is only when they are seen as a critical link between an educational system's inputs and its objectives, outputs, and benefits that they reveal how efficiently and effectively the system is functioning. With this larger perspective, cost analysis becomes a powerful tool to improve the performance and plan the future of any educational system.

In the ensuing chapters we will use several different ways to express and measure educational costs, each with its own particular meaning and utility. These are explained below.

Opportunity Cost (or Sacrifice Cost)

Opportunity cost is the broadest and most fundamental concept of educational costs in the economist's analytical tool kit. Rather than measuring the cost of educational inputs by the prices paid for them, this concept measures them by the value they would have in their most profitable alternative use. The underlying logic of this approach is that, since any nation (or community or individual) has only a limited supply of economic resources to use in any given period, a decision to use some of them for a specific purpose, such as education, means sacrificing the opportunity to spend these same resources on something else.

This may at first strike the noneconomist as a strange way to view costs, yet as individual consumers we do it frequently when we decide to spend our own limited resources on one item rather than on another. To illustrate, suppose you have $25 to spend and are torn between buying a watch and a transistor radio, each costing $25. Since you cannot buy both, you finally choose the radio, but in so doing, you are acutely aware that you have just sacrificed the opportunity to have that watch. To use the economist's jargon, the opportunity cost (or sacrifice cost) of the radio you bought is the

13

value you attach in your personal preference scale to the watch you did not buy.

Or take another example where time rather than money is your scarce resource. You get a day off and would dearly like to go fishing, but your conscience says that you should stay home instead and tend to some much needed household repairs. You face a tough choice here because whichever way you decide will involve a significant sacrifice cost.

This opportunity cost concept, although sometimes difficult to apply statistically, has a variety of valuable uses in educational cost analysis. One such use is that it makes the analyst aware of important economic costs of education that do not show up in the budget or the expenditure accounts, such as the earnings foregone by older students while attending school, the economic value of the "free" broadcast time allotted for educational use, or the yield that the sizable investment in educational facilities could be earning in the most productive alternative uses. All these involve real costs to somebody and to the economy at large, even if not to the education budget. Usually, the sum total of these opportunity costs is substantially larger than the total paid for educational inputs out of the education budget.

This opportunity cost concept is also fundamental to any cost-benefit exercise designed to compare the rate of return on investments at different education levels, and on investments in alternative fields, such as industry. It is also useful to assess the true economic costs of a proposed educational innovation, which may appear quite modest in terms of direct outlays from the education budget, but on closer inspection may involve substantial hidden costs for the community at large and the whole economy.

Resource Costs Versus Money Costs

Educational inputs are expressed in terms of real resource costs when they are measured in physical units, for example, number of teachers or teacher hours, number of textbooks, square feet of floor space. Inputs can also be measured in terms of their monetary value (the price paid for them by the educational system) and expressed as financial or money costs. Both of these ways of expressing input costs are needed in educational cost analysis.

Factor Costs

These are simply the prices paid by education for its various factors of production, that is, for its resource inputs, such as teachers, supplies, equipment, and buildings. Since the prices of different inputs often behave quite differently and are determined by different forces, they must be examined and treated separately when projecting future costs. Factor costs may be expressed either in real or money terms, or in current or constant prices, but to be meaningful, they must be tied to explicit physical and qualitative standards, such as a Grade A teacher, a square foot of floor space, or a gross of writing tablets of a particular size.

Current Costs Versus Capital Costs

Analysts must know whether the expenditure figures being used include capital outlays or cover only current operating costs. The distinction, though somewhat arbitrary, is based on the length of service of various resource inputs. Current costs, by and large, relate to personnel services and consumable supplies that are used up within one fiscal year and must therefore be regularly renewed (hence they are also called recurrent costs or operating costs). Capital costs relate to more durable items (land, buildings, equipment, and so on) that render useful service over a period of years if properly maintained, hence major repairs and maintenance are, strictly speaking, also capital costs since they prolong the useful life of capital items. Initial capital outlays, for example, for a new university, involve large, lump sum expenditures (often financed by loans or grants) and may loom large in total educational expenditures for a particular year. However, when capital items are amortized over their useful lifetime and charged to each year of service, capital costs often turn out to be a relatively modest fraction of total annual costs and of total cost per student.

Total Expenditures

Total expenditures for a given budgetary period are the sum of current and capital expenditures. This total is a rough but useful indicator of the real resource inputs used by an educational system during a given period, particularly when the expenditures are subdivided by categories of inputs, for example, teacher salaries and benefits, other staff costs, instructional supplies, maintenance and repairs, students' boarding costs, construction of new buildings. We say rough indicator advisedly because official budgetary accounts frequently both overstate and understate the real situation, and analysts should therefore use them with caution. A sizable difference often exists, for example, between the approved (or provisional) education budget for the coming year and the actual expenditures during that year. Also, some of the valuable resources used in the educational process are usually not reflected in the budget.

Current Versus Constant Prices

Whenever analysts look at a statistical table showing annual educational expenditures for a series of years, they must determine immediately whether these expenditures are expressed in current prices or constant prices. The difference can be great.

In periods of inflation, total expenditures expressed in the current prices and wages of each year convey an exaggerated impression of the actual increase in real resources going into education. For example, the 1980 budget may be twice as large as in 1970 in financial terms, but if the prices and wages paid by education have risen 50 percent in the interim, then real resources have actually increased by only one-third. Thus analysts must convert the expenditures for each year into constant prices, based on the price and wage structure prevailing in a selected base year. This is best done by applying a deflator, based on an appropriate price index that shows how much prices and wages for educational inputs have increased each year. To take the above example, if the analyst selects 1970 as the base year, its index value would be 100, 1980 would have a value of 150, and the deflator would be 100/150. Applying this deflator to 1980 educational expenditures, which were, say, US $200 million in current prices against US $100 million for 1970, the deflated figure for 1980 (in constant prices) would be only two-thirds of US $200 million, or US $133 million. Thus the real cost increase of 1980 over 1970 has been only 33 percent, not 100 percent as the unadjusted expenditure figures imply.

15

A few caveats are in order about the conversion of current prices into constant prices. First, the results will vary according to the type of price index used. Ideally it should be an index based on the actual mix of physical and human resources purchased by education, which is likely to be different than the mix purchased by other buyers. For instance, teacher salaries may well behave differently in an inflationary period than other wages and salaries in the economy; but since a proper educational index is rarely available, the usual practice is to use a general wholesale or retail (cost of living) price index. This is likely to reduce the accuracy of the conversion somewhat. Second, in developing countries any available price index is likely to be based on urban prices, which differ considerably from prices in rural areas (such as construction costs). This again can reduce the accuracy of the conversion results. Third, the most troublesome problems arise when translating prices expressed in the country's own currency into prices expressed in constant U.S. dollars when making intercountry comparisons. Here a series of technical problems arise, particularly those relating to what exchange rate to use, that can throw off the accuracy considerably.

By the time these various calculations are completed and presented in a neat, printed table, they give the impression of great precision and accuracy, whereas they may reflect a significant margin of error. This is not to say that they are not useful, but that they should be taken with a pinch of salt.

Bearing these caveats in mind, consider the impact of inflation on Algeria's public educational expenditures between 1970 and 1980, summarized in table 2-1. Column 1 shows that total public educational expenditures in current prices increased from 1,854,400 dinars in 1970 to 12,354,500 dinars in 1980, a rise of 566 percent, but how much of this increase was "real" and how much was inflation? To find out, look at the price index in column 2 (in this case the latest year, 1980, was chosen as the base year). This reveals that there was a 125 percent inflation during this period, or in other words, what 44.4 dinars could buy in 1970 required 100 dinars in 1980. Using this index as the deflator to convert the 1970 educational expenditures shown in column 3 into 1980 dinars, we find that educational expenditures in constant prices increased from 4,176,577 dinars in 1970 to 12,354,500 dinars in 1980—a real increase of 196 percent in marked contrast to the apparent increase of 566 percent.

Table 2-1. Algeria: Total Public Expenditures on Education in Current and Constant Prices (1970, 1975, 1980)

Year	(1) Total in Current Prices (dinars)	(2) Price Index (1980=100)	(3) Total in Constant Prices (dinars)
1970	1,854,400	44.4	4,176,577
1975	4,080,500	57.3	7,121,291
1980	12,354,500	100.0	12,354,500
Percentage Increase 1970-80	566	125	196

Source: Summary of unpublished data from UNESCO, Education Finance Division files.

16

Public Versus Private Costs

Public costs are those financed by government, generally on the basis of taxes, loans, and other public revenues. Private costs are those borne by individual students and their families, for example, through school fees and the purchase of uniforms, textbooks, and other supplies, or by participants in nonformal education programs who contribute to the costs, or by private endowments or charitable gifts and grants to either formal or nonformal education. (Government subsidy grants to "aided" private schools or colleges are included in public expenditures and should not be double counted as private costs.) Chapter 4 covers some common statistical booby traps concerning public and private educational expenditures that lie in wait for the unwary planner.

Unit Cost

This is a very useful measurement for many purposes, such as comparing costs between different educational levels, institutions, geographical areas, or times. Such differentials provide important insights that broader composite cost figures conceal.

The most commonly used measurement is the unit cost per student year, calculated by dividing the total expenditure per academic year (either for the whole system or, more likely, for some particular part of it) by the number of students enrolled in the particular educational category. Thus, for example, by properly breaking down overall expenditures, analysts can compute and compare unit costs (per student year) between rural and urban primary schools, primary and secondary schools, secondary general and secondary technical schools, institutions of different sizes, and various university departments.

For some purposes, however, analysts calculate the unit cost per student graduated in contrast to the cost per student enrolled. This is essential, for example, to measure the cost of dropouts and repeaters.

Costs can also be related to a variety of other units, such as teachers, schools, and space. The important thing is that analysts must know at all times precisely what unit is being measured, and remember that it is an average figure for a defined group, which may not be accurate for any one member of the group.

3. Determinants of Educational Costs and Revenues

To give sound guidance to policymakers, educational planners must be able to make realistic projections of future educational costs, and of the revenues likely to be available to cover these costs.[1] To do this, they must understand the main factors that influence educational costs and revenues, how these behave under changing conditions, and to what extent educational decisionmakers and managers can or cannot control them.

The type of systems analysis described in the previous chapter can help planners sort out and examine these various determinants of costs and revenues and shed light on the future by diagnosing the past. Any such diagnosis will reveal the dynamic nature of costs and revenues. All sorts of factors and forces, constantly on the move, combine to determine what it costs to put a youngster through school, his older sister through university, or a parent through a part-time, nonformal training program. The determinants of educational revenues are equally dynamic. For these reasons, educational planners should guard against the simplistic assumption (made too often in the past) that unit costs will remain constant in the future, or that revenues will continue to increase at the same rate as in the past. Such assumptions could put their projections far wide of the mark and mislead policymakers into serious error.

We have chosen to start this analysis on the revenue side of the equation, rather than on the cost and expenditure side, so as to emphasize that the total amount any educational system can spend in a given fiscal period is strictly limited by the funds it has available for that period. Often educational planners have put a major effort into designing an ambitious plan of some sort, only to discover too late that it is simply not feasible within the limits of prospective revenues. At that point the plan must either be abandoned or else sharply cut back in a hurry, using a crude meat axe approach that may destroy its basic balance and integrity. Making a realistic assessment of likely available revenues before putting too much effort into a detailed plan is far better.

---

1   Projections are not predictions. They are simply plausible conjectures of likely future developments based on a diagnosis of recent trends and current factors that are already shaping the future. It is sometimes wise to make high, medium, and low   projections to illustrate the range of possibilities.

Determinants of Educational Revenues

Anyone working in a ministry of education is likely to view the ministry of finance as the main culprit when the amount allocated to the annual education budget is "too small." In reality, however, the fundamental determinants of the education budgets are more complex. Among the most important of these are (1) the rate of inflation, (2) competing demands of other public services, (3) the rate of growth of the national economy, (4) the nature of the tax system and the diversity and elasticity of educational revenues, (5) the ups and downs of foreign trade, and (6) in the case of developing countries, the availability of external assistance.

1. Inflation. Anyone who has been associated with education anywhere in the world since the early 1970s is acutely aware of the havoc that inflation can wreak on educational systems. It robs their budgets of purchasing power and creates serious distortions in their cost structures. It also robs teachers and other educational staff of real income when their salaries lag behind the rising cost of living, as they typically do.

As mentioned earlier, worldwide public expenditures on education increased dramatically between 1960 and 1980, from roughly US $50 billion to nearly US $600 billion, measured in current prices. Unfortunately, a sizable portion of this increase was eaten away by inflation.

The frantic race between educational expenditures and inflation between 1970 and 1982 is illustrated by table 3-1 for a broad sample of developing countries. Take as an example the Democratic Republic of Afghanistan, whose educational expenditures (in current prices) rose by 168 percent between 1970 and 1982 (from an index of 28.3 to 75.9). But during the same period, prices rose by 89 percent (from an index of 55.6 to 104.9), thus wiping out more than half of the apparent increase in educational expenditures. In the case of Bangladesh, the 158 percent increase in public expenditures on education (in current prices) between 1970 and 1982 was entirely offset by a 161 percent rise in prices.

This emphasizes that planners and cost analysts, especially in inflation-prone countries (as in much of Latin America), should keep their eyes open for inflationary tendencies, for even mild inflations can play havoc with educational budgets. Wherever inflationary forces are present, and they surely will be to some extent in the future in virtually all countries, planners should explore the implications of alternative assumptions about the future behavior of prices and wages, and should prepare contingency plans for use in the event of a higher rate of inflation than envisaged by the official education plan. Planners might find it useful to seek the aid of local economists to construct two educational cost indexes, one for the current items (including teacher costs) and the other for capital items, since the two sets of costs often behave quite differently. They should keep these indexes up to date.

Educational cost analysts should bear in mind that education is not merely a victim of inflation; it is often an important contributor to inflation. In many countries, educational expenditures now constitute 15 to 20 percent or more of the total government budget and when, as is usually the case, one of the main causes of inflation is a large excess of government spending over receipts, then education is one of the guilty parties. This is worth remembering the next time the finance ministry's popularity plummets to a new low because it is slashing every ministry's proposed budget in its war

Table 3-1. Public Educational Expenditures Versus Inflation
(Index: 1980 = 100)

Country	Current Expenditures (in current prices)		Percentage increase	Percentage increase in price index
	1970	1982	1970-1982	1970-1982
Bangladesh	40.9	146.4	258	161
Bolivia	2.6	207.5	6,980	2,200
Botswana	5.6	127.4	2,175	126
Burkina Faso	28.3	139.7	484	266
Democratic Republic of Afghanistan	28.3	75.9	168	89
El Salvador	21.7	100.7	364	193
Ethiopia	27.3	131.0	380	46
Haiti	29.2	101.5	248	141
Jordan	14.3	126.9	787	237
Kenya	16.0	120.3	650	221
Madagascar	36.5	109.6	200	328
Malawi	33.7	133.4	295	206
Malaysia	18.5	134.8	629	106
Mexico	6.2	245.9	3,866	941
Morocco	18.4	133.0	623	158
Nicaragua	20.8	186.2	795	370
Pakistan	14.2	136.1	858	280
Panama	32.6	112.0	244	123
Philippines	26.6	133.1	400	307
Republic of Korea	6.4	139.0	2,072	684
Saudi Arabia	46.7	150.6	222	869

Source: Based on data provided by the Statistical Office, UNESCO.

against inflation. Analysts should also remember that an education ministry is not totally helpless when its budget gets cut. This can be a challenge to seek out supplementary income from other sources and to make the available resources go farther by instituting various economies.

2. Competing Demand of Other Public Services. During the 1950s and 1960s, as noted earlier, education in most countries enjoyed a highly favorable budgetary priority that gave it an increasing percentage share of the total public budget and the GNP each year. Predictably, however, this trend could not go on indefinitely without seriously crippling other important public services and dislocating the whole economy.

By the mid-1970s, therefore, the rising curve of education's percentage share of the national economic pie had flattened out in most countries, and in some cases was actually declining. This did not necessarily mean that governments no longer viewed education as important. Rather, it meant that the overall national budget was under increasing stress, and that the claims of other pressing public needs—such as health, agricultural and industrial development, national security, and foreign debt service—had grown more urgent. This situation is unlikely to change substantially in the foreseeable future. In other words, for most countries the halcyon days of the 1950s and 1960s, when education enjoyed an increasing annual share of national resources, are over.

3. Economic Growth. The stabilization of education's percentage share of the total public budget does not mean that the educational budget will necessarily cease to grow. It simply means that its future growth will have to stay more or less in line with the growth of overall public revenues, which in turn will depend in large measure on the growth of the economy. It also means, however, that future annual increments to the education budget are likely to be smaller than previously, leaving less margin for new undertakings, quality improvements, and further expansion. If in the past, for example, the education budget was growing by 10 percent each year against an average annual growth rate of 5 percent in the total public budget (a fairly typical picture), then a reduction to a 5 percent annual increase for education amounts to a sizable cutback.

In these circumstances, educational systems will have only three possible escape routes from a suffocating financial squeeze. First, they can try to find additional sources of income to supplement central government funds, for instance, greater local community contributions, increased private fees and other cost sharing by students and their parents, and special levies on industry for technical education. Second, they can adopt stringent efficiency measures and major innovations designed to reduce unit costs while still permitting quality to rise. Third, they can put the brakes on further expansion of enrollments, especially at the high-cost upper levels. None of these steps will be politically or administratively easy, but the consequences of maintaining a business as usual approach could be far worse.

The important point here is that any future increase in educational expenditures, whether from public or private sources, must come primarily from growth in the national economy. The seemingly small difference between a GNP growth rate of 4 percent and 6 percent a year can readily make a difference of as much as 50 percent in the size of the annual increments to the education budget.

There is a proviso here that educators need to understand very clearly. If a nation is to accelerate its economic growth, it must increase its rate of saving (and decrease its rate of consumption) in order to raise its rate of investment in additional productive capacity—in industry, agriculture, transportation, power, and other fields. Such an increase in "productive investment" is likely, at least for the time being, to be partly at the expense of education, because limited investment funds cannot be used in two places at once. Eventually, of course, the resulting growth of the economy could permit educational needs to be more fully met, though this is of little comfort to the beleaguered educational administrator who has too many eager candidates knocking on the door right now.

It is true, of course, that education itself can lay claim to being an important contributor to economic growth and thus a legitimate petitioner for more investment funds. To grow, an economy must have ample amounts of developed human resources, as well as a favorable institutional, social, and political climate. To the extent that education helps to provide these essentials, which it unquestionably can, it too can be considered a good investment in economic growth.

Educational planners should not press the above too far, however. Insisting that all educational activities and that any amount of additional educational expenditures will contribute more to economic growth than some alternative uses of the same resources is exaggeration. This is plainly not the case. No one disputes that the right kinds of education in the right amounts for the right learners at the right place and time, can make a crucial contribution not only to economic growth, but also to social development and to greater equality. However, education that is inappropriate for the country's circumstances—or the kind that simply goes through the motions but produces little or no real learning—contributes nothing to economic growth (or to anything else for that matter) and may even hinder national development.

4. The Diversity and Elasticity of Educational Revenues. A further important determinant of an educational system's revenues is the diversity of its sources of income and how they react to economic changes. A system that is largely dependent on the central government treasury—which is the case for a great many developing countries—has a large stake in the efficacy of the central government's tax structure. A critical question is how responsive this tax structure is to changes in national income. When a nation's economy grows, say at 6 percent a year, public revenues do not necessarily grow proportionately. They may grow faster or slower, depending on what economists call the elasticity of revenues in relation to national income. When this ratio is less than unity, revenues are "relatively inelastic," meaning that they change at a slower rate than national income. When the ratio is greater than unity, the revenues are "elastic," meaning that revenues overrespond to a change in national income (either up or down).

Obviously, from education's point of view, a revenue structure with a high elasticity is desirable when national income is rising (though not when it is falling). A progressive income tax, for example, is very helpful in this respect, because as individual and business incomes rise, taxes claim an increasing percentage, but progressive income tax laws are still rare in developing countries, and even where they exist are often poorly enforced. Land taxes are much more common, but these unfortunately are among the most inelastic. They tend to lag far behind inflation, real increases of national income, and increases in land value. Consumer sales taxes, payroll taxes, and import and export taxes, also relatively common in developing nations, tend to fall between these extremes.

An important related point is that too heavy reliance on a single source of revenue can lead an educational system down a dead-end street. In the United States, for example, public schools traditionally depended almost entirely on (inelastic) local real estate taxes, but in the period of rapid educational expansion after World War II, this local tax base became a critical constraint. It also resulted in serious educational inequalities between affluent communities and poorer communities. State governments, whose revenues typically came from more elastic consumer sales taxes and income taxes, were obliged to step in and provide a growing share of the support for local schools. Even this sometimes proved inadequate, especially in the lower-income states, and pressures built up for the federal government, with the most elastic tax base of all, to share in school finance, even though, under the U.S. Constitution, education is the exclusive responsibility of state and local governments.

Nigeria's experience is also instructive. Before independence, primary and secondary schools in Nigeria were largely supported by local taxes and private fees and gifts. Immediately after independence, the government rapidly assumed the lion's share of responsibility for school expansion, at first using for this purpose a cocoa stabilization fund that had accumulated over the years. But when the Cocoa Fund was exhausted, schools found their local revenue base weakened and were forced into severe competition with other public services; all of them seeking larger shares of the over-strained national budget.

Later on, when Nigeria's oil boom came along, a portion of the government's profits was channeled into building new universities so that each state would have its own. Unfortunately, these new universities were scarcely off the drawing board when world oil prices tumbled, drastically shrinking federal revenues and leaving the new and partly finished universities stranded.

Developing nations should take note that certain of today's industrialized nations, such as France, that today finance their schools largely from the central government's coffers, did not always do so. It was only as their economy and tax system grew in strength that the central government gradually absorbed more of the expanded educational burden from local communities. Even today, however, state and local taxes and private fees remain a substantial source of educational support in most industrialized nations. Less economically developed nations that concentrate the full financial load of education on the central government too quickly are likely to end up handicapping both education and other public services.

The growing financial crisis of educational systems in recent years makes it clear that if these systems are to have sufficient resources for further expansion and improvement in coming years, they will have to secure supplementary income from private sources, industry, and local government. Only in this way can they broaden and diversify their financial base, improve its income elasticity, and circumvent the revenue bottlenecks that inevitably arise when education depends too heavily on a single source of financial support. This will be essential even if the national economy maintains a high rate of growth. It will be absolutely imperative if it does not.

5. Foreign Trade. Educational systems in developing countries whose economic prosperity and public revenues depend heavily on raw material exports are very vulnerable. Such exports not only sustain domestic employment and income, but earn precious foreign exchange to purchase goods for economic growth, to service foreign debts, and sometimes to meet food deficits. A commodity export tax has the advantage of being relatively easy to administer, but it can also be a very fickle source of revenue. This is especially true in one-commodity countries that rely heavily, for example, on exports of rubber, copper, jute, rice, or coffee whose world price is subject to fluctuations that create a "feast or famine" situation. Even a seemingly moderate swing in the world price can have a multiplier effect (either up or down) on public revenues, national income, and employment levels.

Beyond this, raw material exporting countries tend to experience longer-term worsening of their terms of trade, meaning that the prices they pay for imported manufactured goods gradually increase relative to the prices they receive for their exports, thereby reducing their real purchasing power in world markets. To compound their vulnerability, their particular raw material may be exposed to substitution by new synthetics made elsewhere.

In short, educational systems in raw materials exporting countries that depend heavily on central government revenues are inherently in a precari-

23

ous economic position. Their educational planners and policymakers should keep a sharp eye on international trade trends, for whether their primary school children have textbooks to read five years from now, or their university science laboratories have equipment, may well depend on the price of copper or coffee in markets thousands of miles away. Zambia, whose economic mainstay in the past has been copper, learned this bitter lesson the hard way in recent years as the international price of copper nose dived, and as Zambia's copper reserves showed signs of depletion.

6. External Assistance. External assistance to developing nations coming through multilateral, bilateral, and private channels can have a significant impact on both the revenue and expenditure side of their educational equation.

To be sure, the sum total of aid in any one year generally accounts for only a small fraction of total educational outlays in most developing countries (a number of African nations are exceptions). If well directed, however, such aid can have an importance out of all proportion to its size, particularly by helping to strengthen management capacity, by filling strategic gaps that the recipient nations cannot yet fill themselves, and by supplying research and development resources to initiate needed reforms and innovations. Past external aid, despite its various misfires and other shortcomings, was an important boon to educational development in the 1960s and 1970s, and will continue for a long time to be essential, especially in the least developed countries. Indeed, in certain countries, particularly in Africa, the sudden termination of such aid would cause the partial collapse of whole sectors of the educational system, especially at higher levels where heavy reliance on expatriate teachers cannot be ended quickly.

Experience has also shown that foreign aid is not always an unmixed blessing. In some circumstances, it can seriously distort and disrupt educational plans, raise costs, and place severe strains on local education revenues. This can happen, for instance, when a recipient nation, in anticipation of major outside help, makes substantial complementary investments of its own (it might, for example, build new schools in the expectation of outside help with teacher training and books), but then the outside help does not come through, or it comes through too late to be of maximum use.

A more egregious and all too familiar case is where an outside gift, made with the best of intentions but with too little foresight, ends up costing the recipient nation more than if it had never received the gift. This happens especially when the gift entails transplanting an inappropriate educational model from an industrial country that does not fit the recipient nation's real needs or its pocketbook, and yet thereafter imposes a continuing heavy burden of operating costs on the domestic budget. It also happened many times with so-called pilot projects, whose designers had paid little or no attention to their eventual cost implications for the recipient country. As C. E. Beeby, the eminent international educator from New Zealand once observed, "such pilot projects end up piloting nobody anywhere."

Determinants of Educational Costs

We move now from the revenue side of education's financial equation to the cost and expenditure side, bearing in mind that the ultimate limitation on expenditures in any given period is the total amount of revenues and other resources available for use in that period. We should also bear in mind the important distinction between budgetary costs (which are reflected in the education budget and financial accounts) and *opportunity* or *sacrifice* costs (which reflect the true costs to the economy of the human and material resources used by education, measured in terms of the value they would have in the best alternative uses).

We are concerned here mainly with budgetary costs and expenditures, and with several of their most important determinants, namely, (1) the growth of educational demand, (2) the educational technologies used, (3) the teacher salary structure, (4) dropout and repeater rates, (5) utilization rates, and (6) market forces. Note that (1) and (6) lie outside the education system, beyond the direct control of educational decisionmakers and managers. All the other forces lie within the system and hence, at least in theory and within limits, are susceptible to manipulation and control by educational policies and practices. The latter costs deserve the special attention of cost analysts who are searching for ways to improve the system's efficiency.

1. Educational Demand. The unprecedented growth of educational demand throughout the world since the end of World War II, combined with powerful political pressures to meet this demand, has unquestionably been the greatest single cause of increased costs and expenditures. Several well-known factors have fueled this burgeoning demand, including the "revolution of rising expectations" that swept both the developed and developing worlds; the widespread adoption of national policies to makopportunities available to everyone; the unprecedented growth in population, especially in developing countries; the increased recognition of education's vital role in economic and social development; and the proliferation of new manpower requirements generated by the spread of new technologies, economic growth, and strengthened national and international development policies and strategies.

Continuing increases in educational demand in virtually all countries, though in differing forms and intensity from country to country, are likely to continue in the future. In addition to all the other forces, education creates its own demand, independently of the economy's or the educational system's capacity to fulfill this demand. Youngsters who finish primary school want to continue into secondary school; those who complete the secondary level aspire to go to college or university. Each generation of parents wants their children to have more education that they had, thus the demand continues to escalate.

2. Educational Technologies. In marked contrast to such fields as transportation, manufacturing, agriculture, communication, and health, whose technologies have made spectacular advances in recent times, education's highly labor intensive technologies have not changed radically for generations. This explains why teacher salaries and benefits typically absorb two-thirds or more of the current education budget, and why a decision to reduce class size and the pupil/teacher ratio, or to upgrade the qualifications profile of the teaching staff, can send the unit cost per student and the overall education budget soaring upward.

This situation also helps to explain why education so often finds itself at a competitive disadvantage in trying to recruit and retain able teachers, and

25

why the real cost of education per pupil tends to keep rising without a proportionate increase in quality. These difficulties are bound to continue so long as educational institutions cling to their traditional technologies and practices.

3. Teacher Salary Structures. A further major influence on educational costs is the nature of teacher salary structures, which typically provide for automatic increases based on years of service. Thus, in situations where the recruitment of new teachers at the bottom of the salary scale slows down, causing the existing teacher corps to "age," the average salary and the overall salary bill move upward, even in the absence of any across the board increase in the salary structure.

Teacher salary structures also generally provide for different salary scales based on official teacher qualifications. Thus, fully qualified teachers with the same years of service usually get a substantially higher salary than those with lesser qualifications. The net effect, in any situation where the qualifications profile of the whole teaching staff is steadily improving, is a sizable annual increase in the overall salary bill, even though the salary structure remains constant.

4. Dropout and Repeater Rates. The rapid expansion of enrollments during the 1960s and 1970s was accompanied by a sharp increase in the number of dropouts and repeaters in developing countries, especially in the first four grades. This in turn resulted in much higher costs per completer and a heavy waste of scarce educational resources. The high repetition rate means that the actual time taken by many children to complete a normal six-year primary program is seven or eight years, which has the effect of increasing by one-sixth to one-third the total cost of putting one child through primary school. On top of this, the high dropout rate adds still further to the number of years invested per completer. The recent experience of Honduras, depicted in table 3-2, illustrates the problem. To complete senior high school, for example, theoretically requires a total of 11 successive school years (6 + 3 + 2) at a total cost of 2,920 to 3,330 lempiras per completer; but because of the high dropout and repetition rates, the average number of years invested per completer is actually 18.5, at a total cost ranging from 5,085 to 5,680 lempiras (or 70 to 75 percent higher than the theoretical cost).

So as not to exaggerate the point, note that many dropouts undoubtedly carry away something useful from their unfinished school experience. Yet the great majority, who leave even before gaining permanent literacy, must unfortunately be classified as investments of dubious value. In any event, the objective of the schools is certainly not to produce dropouts; it is to produce "finishers," and by this criterion, their cost-effectiveness ratio must be judged very low. (For a detailed picture of trends in primary school dropout and repeater rates in 121 countries, see UNESCO 1984. This UNESCO study reveals a modest decline in dropout and repeater rates in many developing countries in recent years.)

5. Utilization Rates. The unit cost per student is also substantially influenced by the rate of utilization of teachers and educational facilities and equipment. Many studies have shown that the conventional academic calendar and daily time schedule are enormous wasters of scarce educational

Table 3-2. Honduras: High Cost of Repeaters and Dropouts, 1982/83

Education level	Official duration (years)	Actual years per completer	Theoretical unit cost by education level (lempiras)	Actual/cost per completer (lempiras)
Primary school				
Urban	6	9	990-1,140	1,550-1,740
Rural	6	10	990-1,140	1,720-1,920
"Ciclo comun"	9(6+3)	15 (9.5+5.5)	2,140-2,395	3,735-4,220
Senior high school	11 (6+3+3)	18.5 (9.5+5.5+3.5)	2,920-3,330	5,085-5,680
Technical/ vocational education	12 (6+3+3)	21	5,170-5,575	9,795-10,580
Teacher training	12 (6+3+3)	19	4,810-5,165	7,295-7,910

Source: UNESCO, Education Finance Division, unpublished report, 1984.

resources, especially at the university level where expensive buildings and equipment often stand idle much of the time. Other studies have revealed opportunities to lower costs and improve educational achievements by redeploying students from overcrowded facilities and classrooms to underutilized ones, thus reducing the need to invest in additional facilities and teachers. This is an area where cost analysis has a high potential for discovering ways to improve the cost-effectiveness of educational systems.

6. Market Forces. Like any other buyer, education generally has to pay the going market prices for its various inputs, and usually gets only what it pays for. This is true even when education "sets its own price," as in establishing a teacher salary structure or a cost ceiling on a new building. If education offers an identical salary for humanities teachers and science teachers, but the former are abundant and the latter very scarce, then education can expect to fill its humanities posts with well-qualified teachers (who have few if any better options), but most of its science posts will either go begging or become filled with poorly qualified people.

Similarly, if a school system decides to set a US $800,000 cost limit on a new building that would actually cost US $1,000,000 to build under present market conditions, it will end up either with less of a building for US $800,000 or with no building at all.

In short, education's input prices are generally determined by the interplay of forces in the market or, in the case of centrally controlled nonmarket economies, by government authorities who fix prices for the economy at large and, where necessary, use regulations and controls to ration scarce supplies among competing users.

27

Educational systems have now, however, become "big business" in most countries, and hence major buyers of goods and services. In these circumstances, the system's own buying practices can exert a large influence on certain market prices that both the system and other buyers have to pay. Thus, for example, if the educational system, as the largest buyer of books in a market economy, suddenly doubles its purchases, this could well affect the general market price of books. Prices could move either up or down, depending on the capacity, cost conditions, and degree of competition in the book industry.

Similarly, a large educational construction program, launched at a time when the construction industry is already operating at full capacity, could push up the costs of construction for education and everyone else. Obviously the best time to build is when the construction industry is partly idle and anxious for more business; but education is usually in a hurry and cannot wait for more favorable terms. In many developing countries, the planning of education construction programs has been so poor that implementation has proven impossible at any cost, due to lack of essential materials and equipment.

If education, as a large buyer in the marketplace, acts blindly, it will get a good deal less for its money, but if it is a careful and well-informed buyer and a good negotiator, it can often use its large buying power to get better prices and quality, and thus a maximum for its money. Clever educational purchasing agents can save the system many times their salary, provided they are not too hemmed in by archaic rules and red tape.

Education systems in developing countries need to be especially careful when buying equipment abroad that cannot be supplied locally. They need to shop around and get the best value they can, taking full advantage of competition among supplier nations; but when buying new equipment, education systems need to keep in view the later problem of replacement parts and maintenance. If they get too many different brands of equipment from too many sources, each brand needing its own special replacement parts, they will either have to carry a large inventory of spare parts or risk having equipment idle much of the time while awaiting delivery of parts. Either way, it is a costly affair.

As already emphasized, education is first and foremost a heavy buyer of human services. Being both a consumer and a producer of high-level manpower (unlike other industries, which are simply users), educational systems are inextricably tied to the national manpower market on both their input and output side, and are therefore exposed to major shifts in demand and supply on the manpower scene.

Typical Cost Patterns and Problems

Having examined some major determinants of educational costs, let us look at some typical cost patterns and certain problems associated with them.

Educational costs vary greatly, not only between countries, but within the same country, between formal and nonformal education, and in formal education, between different levels, types, and sizes of institutions, between urban and rural areas, and even within the same institution, between different parts of the curriculum and different points in time. Yet despite these wide-ranging differences in costs, their behavior patterns are often strikingly similar in virtually all educational systems. This is not only because of the influence of certain universal economic principles, but because educational systems the world over operate on the basis of similar structures, technologies, logistics, and underlying pedagogical premises. These factors all have a profound influence on the costs of education, so much so that to achieve any major change in cost behavior is likely to require changing some traditional practices, beliefs, and attitudes.

The Dominance of Personnel Costs

As noted earlier, the salaries of teachers, administrators, and ancillary personnel dominate total educational costs everywhere. This dominance reflects the unchanging labor-intensive character of education's technologies, in contrast to most modern industries.

Developing countries generally spend a higher proportion of their education budgets on salaries than do more developed countries—typically more than 90 percent at the elementary level and somewhat less at the second and third levels. They not only have tighter budgets, but the insistent pressures for more teachers and for higher teacher salaries eat away at provisions for textbooks, supplies, and other current items. In the present climate of increasingly stringent budgets, educational administrators in many countries have found it easier to cut nonsalary costs rather than salary costs, even to the extent in some cases of simply eliminating budgetary allocations for textbooks, supplies, and maintenance. The net effect has been to upset the balance of inputs that most educators consider desirable, thereby handicapping the productivity of teachers and students alike.

The Inexorable Rise of Unit Costs

A second common and related pattern is the long-term rising trend of unit costs for the same type and quality of education. Inflation aside, the real costs of education per student appear to have been on the upswing in many nations for years, and barring major changes in educational technologies, methods, structures, and calendars, they will likely keep rising in the future. Either that, or quality will continue to decline as limited resources are spread thinner and thinner over more and more students.

The main reasons are clear. First and foremost, industries with advancing technologies and hence rising labor productivity set the salary pace for other employers who need similar qualified manpower. Hence educational systems, as major users of such manpower, must keep in step to win a sufficient share of available talent to produce new generations of talent—even if their own labor productivity is not rising. The result is rising costs for the same quality of teachers.

Some important exceptions to this rule have occurred in certain developing countries where initial scarcities of educated manpower and adherence to colonial salary structures after independence (as in Eastern African nations) created a gulf between the wages of common workers and the salaries of teachers. In such situations, however, as the supply of educated manpower expanded, the real salaries of teachers tended to decline relative to average wages and average per capita income, until a more viable balance was reached.

A second cost-increasing factor, as noted earlier, is the cost creep that is built into teacher salary structures in the form of automatic promotion based on years of service. A third force sets in wherever countries seek to restore and improve educational quality by increasing teacher and other inputs per student, for example, by reducing class size and the student/teacher ratio. However, according to some studies of teacher effectiveness, changes in pupil/teacher ratios within a reasonable range do not affect student achievement. Hence, in those developing countries where average staffing ratios are in the range of 30 to 40 pupils per teacher, it would be feasible to increase class size and thereby reduce unit costs without too much damage to educational quality.

Even assuming favorable financial conditions in the future, the long-run outlook virtually everywhere would be for a steady upward march of real unit costs per student, whether or not quality also rose. However, a realistic look at the increasingly unfavorable financial conditions that have besieged most education systems in recent years reveals that something quite different has been happening lately. We find more and more cases where the average cost per student has not been increasing, and in some instances has actually been declining, even in terms of current prices. Usually this is because classes are becoming increasingly overcrowded, the proportion of unqualified teachers is rising, and the provision of textbooks and other essential inputs and support services is declining. In short, administrators are trading quality for quantity, and in some cases, making a mockery of education. In certain instances where the unit cost per student has declined, however, particularly in higher education, this may reflect the attainment of certain "economies of scale."

Higher Costs at Higher Levels

Another common pattern is the marked differential in cost per student between different levels and types of education. As a general rule, unit costs are higher at each successive educational level, and technical education at whatever level is more costly than general education. A linked characteristic is that nonteacher costs become a higher proportion of total unit costs at these higher levels and in technical education.

The large differences between the cost per student in primary education and in higher education in various regions of the world is illustrated in table 3-3. The extreme case is sub-Saharan Africa, where the estimated average cost per higher education student in the mid-1970s was about 100 times the cost per elementary student. In contrast the ratio is much lower in the industrialized countries, with university costs per student year five times the cost of primary unit costs or, in the case of the United States, as low as a two to one ratio. The ratio in the other developing regions is much lower than in sub-Saharan Africa, yet substantially higher than in the industrialized countries.

Several factors account for these differences. In higher education, teachers—and in most developing countries secondary teachers as well—are better paid than primary school teachers and generally teach fewer hours; pupil/teacher ratios are lower; more expensive equipment and larger libraries are required; and there are often sizable room and board costs, scholarship costs, and other student welfare costs. In addition, sending able students abroad on public grants for higher education can be expensive.

Despite these usual explanations, are such wide disparities between the unit costs of primary and higher education really justified, or do they actually reflect a poor deployment and inefficient use of overall educational re-

Table 3-3. Public Expenditures on Elementary and Higher Education per Student, 1976 (in 1976 U.S. dollars)

Region	Cost of higher education (postsecondary)	Cost of elementary education	Ratio of costs of higher to elementary education
East Asia	471	54	8.7
Industrialized Western Countries	2,278	1,157	2.0
Latin America and Caribbean	733	91	8.1
Middle East and North Africa	3,106	181	17.2
South Asia	117	13	9.0
Sub-Saharan Africa	3,819	38	100.5
U.S.S.R. and Eastern Europe	957	539	1.8

Note: The figures shown are avergaes (weighted by enrollment) of costs in the countries in each region for which data are available.
Source: World Bank 1980, p.46.

sources? One of the important functions of cost analysis is to bring such striking facts to light to stimulate re-examination of the causes and justification of unusually high university costs.

Similar searching questions might well be raised about the high costs of technical and scientific training, at both the secondary and tertiary levels. The easy explanation, of course, is that these subjects require smaller classes and more expensive equipment, laboratories, and supplies. But is this the whole story, or even the bulk of it? How does one explain, for example, the paradox that science and technology have done so much to raise human productivity and to lower economic costs in so many other fields, yet have done so little along these lines for education, the academic home of science and technology?

Economies of Scale

In many kinds of educational situations, unit costs decline as the size of the activity expands, up to the point where the economies of scale are exhausted (and where diseconomies of size may set in). This phenomenon of declining unit costs is an important basis for improving the cost-effectivenss of education in a variety of circumstances. Cost analysts should remember, however, that what may be an improvement in economic efficiency may not always be an improvement in educational effectiveness; they should weigh the two sets of considerations against each other and reach an appropriate accommodation.

A case in point is the small village school that has abnormally high costs per student because the student/teacher ratio is so small. A number of countries have consolidated such schools, thereby reducing per student costs, and at the same time enriching and strengthening the curriculum and achieving better learning results. Guinea, for example, established minimum norms for the size of rural schools, aimed at phasing out some 500 "undersized" rural schools by 1984/85. In sparsely settled rural areas, however, there are limits to how far school consolidation can be applied without requiring children to travel unreasonable distances.

31

The need to achieve educational units of an efficient size is even more imperative above the primary level, where the curriculum is broader and more specialized, and requires a more diversified teaching staff and more expensive equipment and facilities. As a general rule, the more advanced the level and the more scientific or technical the program, the larger the institution's size must be to achieve acceptable unit costs and a satisfactory educational program.

A secondary school, for example, or a teacher training college, requires a certain minimum complement of specialized teachers, equipment, library books, and relatively expensive supplies to support a satisfactory curriculum, in contrast to an elementary school where each teacher usually handles a variety of subjects with much simpler equipment. Unless a sufficient number of secondary students or teacher trainees are enrolled in each grade level and subject (such as chemistry, physics, or mathematics) to use fully the capacity of the specialized teachers and facilities, these subjects become too expensive to offer. This helps to explain why many African countries have resorted to secondary boarding schools. Up to a point, it is cheaper to transport day students from a wide area, but beyond a certain radius, boarding facilities become more economical. Boarding is a controversial issue in many countries. Providing boarding involves not only costs, which may become a substantial share of total educational costs, but also important equity questions. Moreover, some advocates of boarding argue that it is qualitatively superior to day schooling because the learning environment is better than in students' homes. Others claim boarding promotes national unity by bringing students from different regions and groups together in schools. There are not any empirical studies of which we are aware that cast light on these matters. What can be done is measure the full cost of boarding and weigh this cost against any assumed gains.

Technical schools present an even greater problem to operate at an optimum scale. A technical school that offers training in several different skills may be impossibly expensive to staff and finance unless enough students are enrolled in each skill area. For example, a recent study of the Trade Training Centers in Guinea estimated that the centers required a minimum enrollment of 540 trainees to allow full use of instructors, whereas in fact all but two of the centers had less than 400 trainees, and most of them had less than 150.

The problem of optimum size presents the greatest difficulties at the university level, especially for small nations. Every nation is understandably anxious to have its own university, and while this is usually feasible for some fields of study, many countries are simply too small and too poor to be able to support first-rate university programs in such expensive fields as medicine, engineering, and advanced laboratory sciences. A solution that makes excellent economic and pedagogical sense (though often unattractive politically), is for small neighboring countries to share common facilities for advanced training and research in these specialized fields. Only in this way can they get quality results at a feasible cost.

The proliferation of uneconomic mini-universities of dubious quality has become a problem for a variety of countries, including some larger ones. Notwithstanding the adverse economic and educational considerations, strong local aspirations and political pressures have often won out. One way in which cost analysis can help in such situations is by identifying those areas of university-level study that could be conducted with reasonable efficiency and effectiveness on a modest scale and thus might form the core of community-level institutions, leaving more costly and advanced studies to the major universities. Even in larger industrialized countries, individual universities are prone to duplicate each other in high-cost specialized fields, resulting in unnecessarily high costs and sometimes poor quality as well.

Economies of scale also apply to school construction. As the experience of the United Kingdom demonstrates, countries can reduce school building costs by the mass production and bulk purchase of standardized components used in the construction of many schools, while still allowing each building to have its own distinctive design (Maclure 1984).

Costs of Mass Media

Economies of scale are critically important when using mass media for educational purposes. The key requirement here is to spread the heavy costs of good program production and transmission over a sufficiently large audience to bring the cost per learner within reach of the education budget. A number of studies have shown how good quality radio instruction—and in some situations even television instruction—can be brought within the economic grasp of developing nations, but also how these powerful, modern educational tools can become an economic liability if they are not well planned and if full advantage is not taken of the potential economies of scale (UNESCO 1977, 1980, 1982; Jameson and McAnany 1978). Such studies have demonstrated repeatedly how an increase in the number of students served can bring down the cost per student dramatically. The example given in table 3-4 relates to Project Minerva, a distance learning system in Brazil that uses radio to provide the equivalent of the last four years of basic education to out-of-school learners. Its total estimated audience in 1978 was 142,000.

Table 3-4. Economies of Scale of a Distance Learning System in Brazil

Number of Students	Average unit cost (1976 cr.)	Average unit cost per subject (1976 cr.)
20,000	674	449
50,000	393	262
100,000	299	199
200,000	252	168
300,000	236	157
500,000	224	149

Source: Oliveira and Orivel 1978.

The Phenomenon of Diminishing Average Costs

Where economies of scale are available, the marginal costs of handling additional students (that is, the cost of each additional student added to the existing system) are lower than the average cost per student for the whole system. This is more than economic jargon; it is a critically important fact of life for anyone who wants to raise the efficiency of any existing educational institution without eroding quality.

We can illustrate the point with a simple example. Suppose that a university with a planned capacity, including faculty members as well as facilities, of 5,000 students has an actual enrollment of only 2,500, and an average cost per enrolled student of US$4,000. The cost of adding 500 more students would obviously be minor—to stretch a point, let us assume it is virtually zero. Adding the 500 would therefore bring the average cost per student down from $4,000 to $3,300. Even then the economies of scale would be far from exhausted, since unused capacity for 2,000 more students is still available. A student body of 5,000 would bring the average cost close to US$2,000.

A number of developing countries that thought they needed to build additional general secondary schools or technical schools to expand enrollments, discovered through surveys of existing institutions that a number of them were operating well below capacity, while a few others were overcrowded. By redeploying students and teachers, they were able to relieve overcrowding and expand total enrollments substantially. In so doing, they held down the average cost per student without impairing quality and, more important, they saved the sizable costs of constructing more buildings and hiring more teachers.

This underscores how important it is for planners to determine the amount of unused capacity in existing institutions before deciding whether and how much new construction the educational system requires. The marginal costs of using present facilities and teaching staff more fully will almost always be substantially lower than the cost of creating and staffing additional new facilities.

Planners should, of course, avoid the illusion that these "bargains at the margin" are limitless. Once existing facilities are used to their full capacity, the cushion for further expansion at low marginal cost is exhausted. Then the marginal cost of adding a still further batch of students suddenly leaps upward because this requires additional new facilities and staff.

School location and population density are crucial factors to consider when expanding a primary or secondary school system into unserved, remote, rural areas. The marginal costs in such situations are likely to be substantially higher than the average cost per student in existing urban schools, due to such factors as the unavoidably small size of primary schools in sparsely populated areas, high transportation or secondary boarding school costs, higher construction costs per student place in rural areas, and special hardship allowances for staff.

Much depends, however, on the definition of capacity. Most education facilities have a considerably greater potential capacity than allowed by traditional academic schedules and customary ways of using facilities.

The High Cost of Traditional Academic Schedules

The typical academic timetable generally results in substantial--sometimes even scandalous—underutilization of expensive educational facilities, and often of staff as well. This is, of course, a touchy subject because the convenience and lifestyles of many individuals are involved, not only administrators and teachers, but students and their families as well. But when, because of budgetary and other resource constraints, the choice comes down to sticking to accustomed practices or giving a larger number of able young people a fair chance at an education, custom cannot reasonably be allowed to stand in the way.

Take, for example, the familiar case of a college that has traditionally held classes in the morning, filled the laboratories and sports fields in the afternoon, and the library in the evening, and shut down for weekends and long holiday periods. A space utilization study of this college would reveal a shockingly low rate of utilization, on both a daily and year-round basis, that would be hard to justify under conditions of serious resource shortages and educational deprivation. Certainly condoning construction of still more buildings to be underutilized in the same fashion would be difficult, hallowed traditions notwithstanding.

One of the greatest wastes, common worldwide, is the well-equipped technical school whose doors close late in the afternoon and are not reopened until the next morning, but that could be profitably used during evenings, weekends, and holiday periods to upgrade workers and supervisors from local industries.

The whole matter of space utilization, academic schedules, and out-of hours use of educational facilities merits close scrutiny by cost analysts and educational managers in virtually all countries. Changes here could often greatly improve the behavior of costs for both formal and nonformal education, as well as provide educational opportunities for more people.

The Impact of Changing Educational Growth Rates on Costs

Many of the points made in this chapter can be knitted together and placed in perspective by examining what happens to the costs of a developing country's educational system when it moves from an initial steady state into a prolonged period of rapid growth, eventually followed by a marked slowdown or even a stoppage in its growth.

For illustrative purposes, consider the education system of Country X, which has moved from colonial status into political independence, and trace what happens to its costs and revenues as it moves through successive phases.

Phase I: Initial State of Equilibrium and Slow Growth

Prior to independence and the onset of accelerated growth, the system is very small. It serves far less than one-quarter of the total primary school-age population, and much smaller proportions of secondary- and postsecondary-age young people, mainly through private institutions. Its annual draft on the nation's resources is also modest, scarcely 1 percent of the GNP. It is a conventional, metropolitan, academically oriented system of generally satisfactory quality. The majority of its graduates become teachers, civil servants, lawyers, or politicians. A few go abroad to study medicine and other advanced specialties, and some never return. The system supplies hardly any manpower to the industrial, commercial, or agricultural sectors.

At this point, the system is as close to a state of equilibrium as it is ever likely to get, both internally and in relation to its economy and society. Its pyramidal enrollment structure and its student flows from primary to secondary to higher education are in good balance, and its dropout and repeater rates at each level are considered wholesome—just high enough to accom-

35

plish the classical weeding out job. The supply of newly trained teachers is well matched to annual replacement requirements and to the very modest rate of enrollment expansion. The qualifications profile of the teaching force is high; only a small fraction of elementary teachers are technically unqualified, but they have been carefully chosen and are being upgraded. Physical facilities are adequate; occasionally an old building needs replacement or a new one needs to be added, but in most years, the main capital outlays are for maintenance and repairs. The same is true for instructional materials; the supply of textbooks is adequate, but a portion needs replacing each year.

The schools are in good standing with the people and the government; not everyone attends school who would like to, but the political pressures to enlarge admissions are far from intolerable. The graduates at each level get appropriate jobs with little difficulty because their limited supply is in good balance with the employment demand.

What do educational costs look like under this condition of equilibrium? The general level and structure of costs, and their relationship to one another, have been relatively stable for years, though drifting upward. Overall expenditures rise 3 to 5 percent annually (in constant prices), reflecting mainly a gradual rise in average cost per student, which in turn reflects mainly an upward drift in average cost per teacher. The rest of the increase is largely accounted for by a slow expansion of enrollments. The division of total expenditures between primary, secondary, and higher education has remained fairly stable. So has the ratio of unit costs per student between levels, though the unit costs of the new university college have been creeping up faster than other levels. Capital costs are a minor item compared to recurrent costs, except for years when a new building is constructed.

Phase II: Rapid Growth Sets In

For familiar reasons—the country gains its independence, the youth population rises, human aspirations are unleashed, and national development is emphasized—the system suddenly finds itself hit by a sharp rise in educational demand and the need to embark on a major expansion, which in ten years will more than double its size. The new tidal wave of students first hits the elementary schools, but soon washes into secondary and higher education.

Shortages quickly become the order of the day—shortages of classrooms, teachers, textbooks, laboratories, equipment, and supplies—shortages of everything but students. The system's first response is to expand class size, to find provisional classroom space, and to hire large numbers of "temporary," unqualified teachers. Only later does a major expansion program get underway to build more classrooms, and even later to train more teachers. The pressures grow for teacher salary increases as an expedient way to improve teacher supply, but despite such increases, the qualifications profile of the teacher corps continues to decline. Meanwhile, concern mounts about the erosion of quality and the sharp upswing of dropout and repeater rates. For some years, graduates from each level encounter a vigorous employment market, but eventually it starts to decline, first for primary school leavers, and then for secondary and postsecondary graduates.

What is happening to educational costs now? Initially, overall the system's recurrent costs have risen at roughly the same rate as enrollments,

36

about 10 percent per year; but after a time costs rise faster than enrollments. Meanwhile, capital outlays become a much higher proportion of the budget than ever before.

Behind these aggregate cost movements, some very interesting developments are taking place. At the elementary level, unit costs per student actually decline somewhat at first, thanks to the increase in pupil/teacher ratios and class size, and to the hiring of many young, unqualified teachers at the bottom of the salary scale. But eventually the unit costs start moving upward again, reflecting salary increases, the aging and automatic promotion of these younger teachers, the upgrading of many to a higher qualification level, and the stabilizing of class sizes (now large). In other words, the initial economies of scale, mainly through enlarged class size, and the lower costs resulting from the heavy use of unqualified teachers, have now been exhausted and the cost-increasing forces have taken over. Paradoxically, even as unit cost per enrolled student was declining, the cost per completed student was rising rapidly, due to the sharp increase in dropout and repeater rates.

So long as primary education was expanding substantially faster than secondary and higher education, the comparatively lower cost of primary schooling held down the system's average cost per student. As the accelerated expansion of enrollments shifted toward the higher levels, the average cost per student rose disproportionately.

After 15 years of rapid expansion, the system's total enrollments more than doubled, and total public expenditures on education more than quadrupled, thus becoming a much increased percentage of the GNP and total public expenditures. The equilibrium the system started with has now been shattered, and things are still very fluid.

Phase III: A Turning Point is Reached
This new phase is marked by a major shift in the relationship between the educated manpower supply and the employment market. The enlarged output of the education system and the return of many students who have graduated from foreign universities has greatly improved the nation's supply of high- and middle-level manpower. However, all positions that were hard to fill just after independence, especially in government and education, have now been largely filled, albeit often with underqualified people. As a result, the earlier worries about manpower shortages are now turning into worries about the mounting educated unemployed.

The one bright spot for educational administrators is that the back of the teacher shortage has finally been broken except in a few fields, especially in the sciences and technical subjects. Teacher training capacity and output has finally caught up with demand and, ironically, the new question is whether too many teachers will be produced.

The schools certainly could use more teachers, both to reduce the inflated pupil/teacher ratio and overcrowded classes, and to handle further expansion of enrollments; but a grave new problem looms. The government's budget has by now become seriously overstrained and debt laden, and the competition for public funds for other sectors—especially agriculture, health, and the military—has intensified. Hence expanding the education budget each year is getting harder. A few years ago, winning a 10 to 15 percent increment annually was not too difficult, but now even 5 percent

37

has to be fought for hard. To make matters worse, unit costs are now rising even faster as the teacher corps regains a more normal age distribution and its qualifications improve, and any progress toward reducing oversized classes simply makes unit costs per student rise even faster.

Thus we find a new cost configuration. Average costs per teacher and per pupil are both rising steadily, even though many classes are still oversized and textbooks remain scarce. The former gap between cost per primary teacher and per university teacher is narrowing somewhat as primary teachers become better qualified. Capital costs continue to run high as new facilities are created, but each new building imposes high recurrent costs on future budgets, and by now the cumulative effect of previous new construction is enormous.

Phase IV: Expansion Slows Down or Halts

At thisstage, which is where the bulk of developing countries found themselves in the early 1980s, little choice is available except to curtail drastically the dramatic educational expansion that had been going on for two decades. The dominant factor now is not a shortage of potential teachers, and certainly not of students; it is primarily a financial problem created by the relentless pressure of rising costs against increasingly stubborn budget ceilings.[2]

What happens to costs under these circumstances, and to the quality of education? Much depends on the policies adopted with respect to basic reforms and innovations, internal economies, admission standards, and teachers.

If the country pursues "normal" practices, the educational system will surely get deeper and deeper in the hole, both economically and educationally. In all likelihood, oversized urban primary classes will grow even larger, and rural schools will lag even further behind in quality and have even fewer textbooks, along with continuing with high dropout and repeater rates. Secondary schools and universities will become increasingly bloated, and the quality and relevance of education up and down the line will continue to erode.

If, however, educational managers take imaginative and courageous steps to overhaul the system so as to improve its orientation, relevance, efficiency, and viability, to establish stricter admission standards for higher education, and to adapt the system's output mix (particularly in high-cost

---

2   The situation of the industrialized countries was quite different. Their educational expansion slowed drastically in the 1970s, including actual declines in elementary and secondary school enrollments, and the overall expansion came to a virtual halt by the end of the decade. The main cause, however, was not financial, though they all experienced increasingly difficult educational financing problems. Rather, the stagnation of enrollments was due primarily to the sharp drop in birth rates around the mid-1970s, which dramatically differentiates the developed and developing nations in the 1980s and 1990s. The industrial nations had also achieved high participation rates by the late 1970s, especially in primary and secondary education; hence the earlier pressures for expansion had largely subsided.

fields) to prospective employment opportunities, then perhaps the system can endure the rough weather ahead, especially if it gets a reasonable amount of external assistance of the right kind and uses it well.

In either of these scenarios, however, teacher costs are almost bound to rise, even in the absence of a general salary increase over and above inflation. This is because with curtailment of recruitment of young, new teachers at the bottom of the salary scale, the existing staff will progressively age and move up the automatic salary scale, thus steadily increasing the average cost per teacher. The only alternative is a policy that forces down the real incomes of teachers by not adjusting their salaries to offset inflation. Such a policy, however, is hardly an effective way to preserve and enhance quality and relevance or to inspire enthusiasm among teachers for implementing major reforms and innovations.

4. Doing Your Own Cost Analysis

This chapter offers some suggestions on how to start applying cost analysis to your own situation. Obviously we cannot consider each and every possible use of educational cost analysis, but we can offer suggestions, caveats, methodologies, and illustrations that are relevant to a wide range of uses and circumstances, and that you can adapt as required.

The practical application of educational cost analysis involves more than simply knowing the appropriate concepts and analytical methods. It also involves choosing the right approach and maintaining good human relations; knowing where and how to get the necessary basic data and how to judge the reliability of different sources; allocating your time judiciously; avoiding certain conceptual and accounting pitfalls; and skillfully arranging trade-offs between economic, pedagogical and other considerations Although the examples in this chapter are taken mainly from formal education, the basic principles and methods involved also apply to nonformal education.

Getting off to a Good Start

Your first cost analysis assignment may well be a crash operation. Perhaps the deadline for submitting the new draft education plan is close at hand, but it must first be costed and its feasibility tested; or a project proposal must be prepared for a mission from the World Bank scheduled to arrive soon; or a major decision on salary policy is pending, but its economic implications must first be determined. If you are lucky, you will have previously had a chance to explore costs in your education system in a general way, but this would make you an exception to the general rule.

In all events, getting started right is half the battle. By honoring the following simple rules you can save much time, avoid many difficulties later, and increase the ultimate impact of your efforts.

Clarify Your Objectives at the Outset

Before you get too committed to a particular approach or buried in a mass of statistics, take the time to define clearly the objectives of your exercise and the key questions you will seek to answer. Be sure that your objectives are relevant to the important issues requiring decisions.

You may find it useful to ask yourself such questions as these: What are the most critical emergent problems confronting this educational system that cost analysis might help to clarify and solve? What experts on the scene could contribute to an analysis aimed at solving these problems? Who in particular might be interested in the results of such cost analysis and could use them effectively? How and when can the results best be entered into the decision-making process so they will have a maximum impact on what is decided? In what form should I present the final results to be of greatest effect?

Consult Your Main Clients at an Early Stage

The best way to answer the questions and to guarantee that your efforts will be worthwhile is to involve the users of your analytical results at the start. These users include the managers and decisionmakers who need the help of cost analysis and who can put the results into action. Ask them what they see as the main problems and questions that need attention. You may not agree entirely with them, and perhaps you can gently persuade them that even more important questions need answering initially, but in all events, take their views seriously and meet them more than half way. Not only may they have more experience than you, but without their interest and cooperation you may not get very far.

You may, of course, run up against some clients who are so skeptical of cost analysis, or who feel so threatened by it, that they are not prepared to cooperate with you. If so, the burden of proof will be on you. The best tactic in such circumstances is not to write such people off as "the enemy," but to do your diplomatic best to persuade them to reserve judgment until you have had a chance to demonstrate how cost analysis might help them.

Find Some Able Collaborators

As early as possible, identify some technical collaborators who have skills and access to sources of information that supplement your own. They may include, for example, an educational statistician and an experienced budget officer in the education ministry, a personnel manager in the civil service directorate, a general economist at the planning commission interested in human resource development, a manpower expert at the ministry of labor, a demographer at the university or the census bureau, a fiscal expert in the ministry of finance, and a construction cost estimator in the ministry of works.

Things usually move faster and more smoothly, especially in the early stages, if this sort of collaboration is kept as informal and unstructured as possible. To try right at the outset to set up a formal interministerial committee to deal with technical and information matters often wastes time, creates needless bureaucratic problems, and worst of all, jeopardizes the essential climate of informal give and take among colleagues.

Thus to be a successful cost analyst, you must not only be technically competent, but be able to work well with others in an atmosphere of professional objectivity and mutual respect, regardless of traditional bureaucratic obstacles to easy communication.

Use a Systems Approach

To identify all the key questions that your inquiry should answer, whatever its objectives, a useful approach is to use the broad perspective that systems analysis provides.

To illustrate, suppose that your first assignment is to cost a proposed new teacher training project whose aim is to increase the supply of fully qualified teachers and thus upgrade the qualifications profile of the teacher corps. Since an international capital loan is being considered, you will naturally want to give careful attention to the capital costs involved, but it would be a grave mistake to stop there. The most important issue is not whether your government can qualify for the loan, but whether, if it gets the loan, it can afford the subsequent annual cost consequences.

The questions thus posed go beyond capital cost analysis, for example: What will the annual operating cost of this new teacher training project be? What effects will this project have on the future teacher salary bill and other recurrent costs? Can the country afford the project without seriously penalizing other educational activities? Is this the best way to upgrade the teacher corps, or are there alternative ways to achieve the same result more quickly, cheaply, and effectively? Finally, taking a longer view, is the country risking overexpansion of its teacher training capacity? Once the immediate backlog of demand for trained teachers is met, will the annual demand settle down at a lower level, leaving underutilized, expensive training capacity?

As this illustration shows, there is no such thing as a narrowly circumscribed, isolated problem for cost analysis. Any problem is part of the seamless web of interconnecting elements that can only be seen in proper perspective through the wide-angle lens of systems analysis.

Once you have identified your objectives and key questions and mapped out your approach, you will begin in earnest the search for pertinent facts. If you have just joined the educational management team from some other field, you may be astonished at how few hard facts are available to assess the system's performance and to plan its future. In some cases, however, you may be surprised by the variety and quality of data available at the individual school level or in the regional educational offices when the central office lacks an adequate data base. Collecting facts from scattered sources is likely to take more time and effort, but the results will usually be worth it.

Whatever your circumstances, do not be discouraged; cost analysis can be helpful. The less adequate and less sophisticated the data you have to work with, the more ingenious and sophisticated you will have to be in using them to best advantage. Also, the more frequently you will have to substitute judgments and "guesstimates" for hard facts.

Minimum Essential Facts and Critical Ratios

Even though no magical list of the minimum essential facts needed for cost analysis in all places and for all purposes exists, in any situation you will be severely handicapped if you do not have at least the following statistics, preferably for each of the past five years or more:
- *total enrollments* broken down by levels and types of institutions, geographic areas, and if possible, by individual grade levels;
- *annual number of completers* in each category of institutions (surprisingly, these figures are often not easily available, especially for primary education);
- *annual number of dropouts* and *repeaters* (shown separately) by level, grade, type of institution, and geographic area;
- *total number of teachers*, distributed by type of institution and level, and broken down if possible by subject area, qualification level, years of service, salary categories, and status (full-time, part-time);
- *total annual expenditures* on each level and type of institution, broken

down by recurrent and capital costs and by major subcategories within each of these (particularly teacher costs separated from other recurrent costs, and new construction and equipment from repairs, maintenance, and replacements);

• a breakdown of *annual revenues* by sources of finance (for example, central and local government, private grants and fees, foreign aid) for each main education sector.

In addition to these more or less standard educational statistics, cost analysis and planning require much information on economic and social trends of a sort that educational administrators have not been accustomed to using. This includes data on the growth and composition of national income and public revenues; population growth, migration, age and geographic distribution; manpower requirements and employment trends and prospects; general price, wage, and construction cost trends (by urban and rural areas); and changes in the structure of the economy and the labor force. Such data are usually available in some form in various government bureaus. Other valuable sources include *UNESCO Statistical Yearbooks* and various special UNESCO reports, the World Bank's annual *World Development Report*, the International Monetary Fund's *Finance and Development* periodical, and the United Nations demographic reports.

Inevitably the various facts and estimates contained in your presentations will vary greatly in precision and reliability. Do not be apologetic or embarrassed about making crude and approximate estimates if that is the best the situation allows, but always be candid about it. Policymakers must be aware of the possible margin of error in any set of estimates you give them so that they will not treat them as scientifically revealed truths if in fact they are only rough approximations. Remember also that even where more refined estimates might be possible, rough and ready ones are often sufficient for answering broad questions. To embellish them further would go beyond the point of diminishing returns and be a poor use of your time. Finally, to cover the above situations, we suggest that you adopt a scale of accuracy ratings and attach to each set of figures you circulate an estimate of accuracy. This will help those who use your findings to make due allowance for whatever margin of possible error they may contain.

Beyond the basic statistics listed above, a number of crucial relationships, indicators, and patterns are invaluable for a variety of purposes. Where possible, gather them for the past five years or more to reveal significant trends and shifts. Some can be derived from combinations of aggregate statistics, while others require sample studies of institutional accounts and performance. Among the most important are:

• the ratio of educational expenditures to the GNP and to total public expenditures (including all levels of government);

• the ratio of teacher costs to total recurrent costs, by education levels;

• the comparative level and composition of unit costs per student in rural versus urban schools;

• the comparative cost per student in primary, secondary, and postsecondary education, for different types of institutions, and for urban and rural areas;

• the comparative cost per student of day schools and boarding schools;

• the comparative unit and overall costs of formal technical schools versus nonformal training schemes;

43

• the theoretical cost of a primary school graduate (cost per year x normal number of grades) as against the actual cost per graduate (allowing for dropouts and grade repeating);

• the comparative costs and composition of undergraduate and postgraduate university students, broken down by major fields of study;

• the pupil/teacher ratio and class sizes in different types of institutions and in various subjects;

• the utilization rates of staff, facilities, and equipment for various types and levels of institutions.

Unit cost figures and ratios such as these do for the educational diagnostician what x-ray photos and blood tests do for the medical diagnostician; they reveal what is going on internally, how the patient is faring, and what remedial action the patient may need.

When studying the foregoing indicators, you may find it useful to compare them with norms that have been established on pedagogical or other grounds to see if there are any substantial deviations. You may find, for example, that class sizes in rural primary schools are often far below the pedagogically acceptable norm, thereby revealing possibilities for achieving economies by raising class size through school consolidation or multi-grade teaching. Similarly, you may find that sizable economies and better learning results can be achieved in colleges and universities by enforcing reasonable norms pertaining to staff/student ratios, staff/student contact hours, and the ratio of senior to junior staff. We know of one African university where some years ago, a staff utilization survey revealed that instead of the authorized staff of 208 people, 300 were on the staff. Most of the excess staff were from abroad and were not shown in the official budget or staff establishment, yet they were teaching and doing research. In an opposite situation, such a survey might reveal that the staff was so small relative to the large number of students that the institution was simply going through the motions of providing a university education.

Strengthening the Information System

While you are struggling to extract the best answers from the partial evidence at hand, you should also try to strengthen your information system for the future. But beware the statistician who considers that all statistics are equally important. Some are vital, some are useful but not essential, and still others have too little value to justify the cost of collecting them. Thus, a cost-benefit mentality is important when selecting the statistics that you should give priority to when improving an educational information system. The first thing to ask is: What are the most critical questions that educational managers need answered, and what facts are essential to provide these answers? Unless you approach the matter in this fashion, you can waste a lot of time collecting data that are of secondary importance and may go unused, while you bypass certain essential facts.

Once you have sorted out the different categories of statistics according to their relative importance for decision making and management, you have two other questions to ask: When will you need each particular set of facts? Must you collect them from all educational units or will a sample suffice?

Too often limited data gathering resources are dissipated on a full census approach instead of relying for some purposes on well-chosen samples. Obviously, to get reliable annual totals of enrollments, teachers, classrooms, graduates, and the like, you will have to obtain data regularly from every educational unit. You will not have to collect all of it yourself, however. In some case, you can find adequate data in one or another specialized central bureau (such as data on teachers in the civil service directorate). If, however, you want to monitor dropouts and repeaters, for example, or to check the comparative unit costs of different levels and categories of educational institutions, you can do it better and cheaper by using a sample.

The sampling method, however, must be used with sophistication or the results can be very misleading. Especially important is selection of a truly representative sample that gives proper weight to each category of schools or higher institutions under study. Take care when designing questionnaires or interview forms to ensure that the resulting data are comparable and unambiguous. If, for example, you want to study the comparative costs of different types of secondary schools, do not load your sample with prestigious schools near the capital just because they are convenient to visit and keep better records. A true picture requires a cross-section appropriately weighted to represent different types of secondary schools, for example, different sizes, day and boarding schools, rural and urban, academic and vocational, private and public, boys, girls, and coeducational schools, and any other relevant classifications.

Strengthening an educational system's information base and regular flow of essential facts about the system's performance is one of those tasks for which external technical assistance may be especially helpful. However, if your government decides to request such assistance, be sure to insist on the right kind of expert. The right kinds are those who are not simply statistical experts with impressive university credentials, but those who appreciate the practical needs and problems of educational managers. In addition, they should be experienced in working with other countries, and thus well aware of the limitations and obstacles to gathering reliable data from the field. Good experts should also be able to train local personnel to run the improved information system after their contracts expire.

Limitations of Central Budgets and Records

The first data source that you would probably turn to is the central education budget and financial accounts. If yours is a highly centralized educational system, you would start by going to the appropriate office in the national ministry of education to examine the budgetary expenditure records and other central records on teachers, enrollments, facilities, and so forth. If you are working in a decentralized system, as in India, Brazil, or Nigeria, you may have to travel further and aggregate data from a combination of national, state, district, and even local accounts.

An important caveat here is that when using budgetary accounts, take year-end figures of actual expenditures rather than beginning of the year projections or authorizations. A budget, after all, is only a forecast of things to come, and until they have actually come and gone, the figures shown are purely hypothetical. Wide disparities between the authorized budget and the year-end picture of actual expenditures are not uncommon.

Whichever set of figures you use, however, be consistent or you will end up with erroneous comparative figures over a period of years.

Official accounts and records can be a rich and convenient source of data, but they also have serious limitations and pitfalls. Often they conceal as much as they reveal because they deal in broad aggregates and averages that hide cost and expenditure differentials of great importance to cost analysts. For example, they may yield useful data for tracing broad expenditure trends, but insufficient data to compute many of the critical ratios and differentials listed earlier. Moreover, the ministry of education's budget never includes all of the nation's expenditures on education, such as government funds spent on nonformal education by various ministries and, of course, private expenditures (which can be very sizable in the aggregate). At the same time, the ministry of education's budget may include certain noneducational items, such as public museums, libraries, and special cultural projects.

A further limitation is that public (and also private) education accounts are usually broken down into expenditure classifications that are not very meaningful for certain important cost analysis purposes. Typically they show expenditures by object (for example, salaries, utilities, supplies, equipment), but not by function or program objective. Thus, for instance, the budget accounts may reveal the aggregate costs of teachers or supplies for primary schools, but they fail to disclose how much was spent respectively for teaching reading, writing, arithmetic, or a foreign language. Such cost breakdowns are important for assessing the cost effectiveness of the schools in these different subjects.

Bear in mind that conventional education budgets were designed to serve the purposes of appropriations bodies and auditors, not the more precise needs of educational planners and managers. Members of a legislative committee, for example, can tell from the budget how much more (or less) of the taxpayers' money the schools are spending this year than last year, but they cannot tell for what specific educational purposes the money is being spent, what results are being attained, or whether society is getting full value for its money. Similarly, government auditors may be able to catch a thief by examining the budget accounts, but they are not likely to catch blatant inefficiencies in the educational system without more information and investigation.

What it all comes down to is that cost analysis of the sort discussed in this book has not been of great concern to most educational administrators until recently. Now that it has become absolutely essential because of unyielding budget ceilings, budgetary accounts will have to be modified and amplified to serve these new purposes as well as the old ones. This does not mean throwing out the old accounting system and budget reports that everyone is familiar with and that serve some useful purposes. Rather, in most cases it means supplementing the customary accounts and reports with new ones that provide additional insights essential for effective planning and management. An encouraging sign is that many educational systems and institutions have already begun remodeling and supplementing their basic records and accounts so as to reveal much more about the performance of the system than ever before.

Apart from budgetary accounts, other types of central records are also of great value, if they are well kept. They include, for example, data on enrollments and completions by year, information on teachers broken down by specialty and by employment category, and detailed records on facilities. Education systems vary greatly, however, in the extent and detail of such central records and in how well they are maintained. Earlier studies by the IIEP showed, for example, that relatively few systems had the detailed central records on teachers necessary to project teacher costs with reasonable accuracy or to discover, for example, that technical teachers were so badly allocated that some schools were seriously understaffed while others were grossly overstaffed. In one case, a field study of individual institutions revealed a great disparity between what the central files showed about the condition and use of individual secondary school facilities and equipment, and the actual conditions.

In summary, official educational records on expenditures, enrollments, teachers, and facilities are usually the richest single source of data, but they do not suffice for all purposes and can often be very misleading. You will surely find, if you have not already, that to answer certain key questions concerning the real unit costs and the use of staff and facilities, as well as the wide discrepancies between schools or other institutions in the same category, there is no substitute for getting out and doing an on the spot survey of a good sample of them. The result will often be startling.

Pitfalls to Avoid

In measuring today's costs or projecting tomorrow's, you can easily get into trouble unless you are clear at all times about what costs and whose costs you are trying to measure, and unless you are careful to include all the appropriate costs. A few tips to help you follow.

Full Costs Versus Partial Costs

As indicated earlier, education budgets, whether public or private, never reveal the full costs of education to the economy at large. The public budget of the national ministry of education invariably excludes (1) all private costs, (2) the costs of education and training activities (including many nonformal ones) conducted or supported by other governmental agencies, and (3) the financial contributions to education by lower echelons of government. It may also omit (4) certain costs of formal education within the jurisdiction of the education ministry that are actually carried on the budgets of other governmental agencies, such as contributions to teacher pensions, teacher housing costs, student dormitories, or utility costs, and (5) educational expenditures supported by external funds. Thus, if you are trying to measure the full costs of education supported by public funds, you will have to search beyond the national education budget and extract appropriate items from other public budgets as well.

A recent report on Tanzania relating to 1983/84, includes an unusually comprehensive breakdown of budgeted "development expenditures" (as distinct from regular recurrent expenditures) for a wide variety of governmental educational and training institutions and programs, both formal and nonformal. The more than 40 specific programs listed include not only the ministry of education's activities, but also those coming under 14 other ministries, the prime minister's office, and subnational regions. In each instance, the report shows the total budgeted expenditure, broken down between domestic funds and external funds.

47

Table 4-1. Tanzania: Budgeted Development Expenditures on Education and Training, 1983/84 (thousands of Shillings)

Responsible agency	Budgeted expenditure	Local funds	External funds
Ministry of education	268,300 (48.4%)	101,517	166,783
Other ministries and departments	222,878 (40.2%)	98,765	124,113
Regions	62,926 (11.4%)	45,620	17,306
Total (56.0%)	554,104 (100.0%)	245,902 (44%)	308,202

Source: UNESCO, Education Finance Division, unpublished report.

The summary figures in table 4-1 are very revealing. Surprisingly, the ministry of education accounts for only 48 percent of the total budgeted development expenditures on education and training. This demonstrates the important point that nearly all government ministries and departments in developing countries are significantly involved in education and training (much of it nonformal). Another significant point is that external funds in the Tanzania case account for over half the development expenditures, indicating the strategic importance of external assistance for education and training in many African countries. (External funds, however, generally account for a much small percentage of total recurrent costs in these countries.)

As the Tanzanian example demonstrates, if you want to measure the full financial costs of education supported by public funds, you will have to search beyond the national education budget and extract appropriate items from other public budgets as well. If you want to go even further and measure the country's total expenditures on education, you will in addition have to collect data on or estimate expenditures by students and their families (for example, on school fees, uniforms, books and supplies, transportation, room and board), and by private educational institutions (being careful not to double count government subsidies to private schools).

For most purposes, however, you will not need to include all these financial costs of education, but even when you do, you can use rough estimating methods for some of the smaller elements. What is important is that you know when you are omitting something and that you make your clients aware of it.

Budgeted Costs Versus Opportunity Costs

As explained in chapter 2, when an analyst takes opportunity costs into account, the results frequently reveal a substantially larger real cost of education to the economy than is revealed by the education budget. A case in point is the income earning opportunities foregone by working age students while attending school or college. The magnitude of this particular opportunity cost depends, of course, on the condition of the employment market and the extent to which it could provide jobs to these students if they were not in school.

In poor families, there is often an important linkage between the opportunity cost of children attending school and high dropout rates. In such circumstances, the opportunity cost to the family means that even eight- to ten-year-old children must do their part to help the family survive, for example, by tending animals or younger siblings while the mother works outside the home; by doing housework for a more affluent neighbor in return for a midday meal; by helping the parents with farm work; or by scavenging or begging for food and other essentials. Sending the children to school can involve a substantial sacrifice for the family, even more so if it also requires cash outlays for school fees, uniforms, textbooks, and other supplies.

For most purposes, however, working with financial costs, and even with institutional budgetary costs, is sufficient. However, you should bear the opportunity cost notion in mind, particularly when considering the true costs of education to the economy. This would be the case, for example, in doing a broad cost-benefit study that seeks to differentiate the social benefits accruing respectively from primary, secondary, and university education. It would also be the case when economic planners and top authorities are trying to achieve a more or less optimum allocation of scarce resources between education and other sectors.

Costs to Whom?

As you can see from the foregoing, you should always ask yourself: Whose costs does this particular analysis deal with? Is it concerned only with financial costs to the central government, or to all levels of government combined, or with private financial costs as well? Is it concerned only with financial costs, or with the full, real costs to the economy? Is it concerned only with costs to the domestic economy, or to foreign economies too? The latter distinction becomes important where foreign aid is a big factor. For example, in examining the overall educational expenditures of certain African countries whose educational systems are heavily dependent on external assistance, you must know to what extent the figures include or exclude such assistance; otherwise you cannot properly assess the true burden on the local economy and taxpayers.

Donor Costs Versus Domestic Value

Here you should remember the difference between the cost of foreign aid to a donor nation and its economic value to the recipient country. The cost to the donor country is measured in terms of its prices, wages, and salaries and usually includes substantial transport and other special costs. The value of the particular item of aid to the recipient country, however, should be measured in terms of that country's economy, and what it would cost to provide that item locally without help.

Take the case of a Peace Corps teacher who is sent to an African country. Let us suppose (1) that the total cost of this volunteer teacher to the United States, including training, transportation, living allowances, and so on, averages out to US$12,000 per year; (2) that the host government pays US$500 per year toward the teacher's local maintenance; and (3) that the total cost of an equivalent local teacher (if available) would be US$2,000 per year. From the point of view of the host country, the real value of the aid received in the form of this teacher is US$1,500 (US$2,000 minus US$500), despite the fact that the cost to the donor government was much higher.

This same proposition holds with respect to capital assistance. A new technical school, fully equipped, might cost a donor nation US$2,500,000 (using its own equipment and professional manpower), but the recipient government might have built and equipped an equivalent facility for only $1,500,000 (using entirely domestic personnel and materials at local prices and shopping in the world market for the best buys on equipment).

Hidden Costs

Whether you are dealing with the public or private costs of education, or with domestic or foreign costs, you must keep an eye out for hidden costs that are not reflected in the financial accounts. Certain of the unbudgeted private costs mentioned earlier, such as family outlays for books, uniforms, school meals, and transportation, are hidden costs. In the African university example cited earlier, the salaries and other costs of the foreign professors who were rendering teaching and research services but were not included in the university budget or the official staff establishment, were important hidden costs. A very common hidden cost these days is the "free" broadcast time received by schools or by nonformal education programs from private or public radio or television stations for instructional programs. The service may be free so far as the school or nonformal education budget is concerned, but it is a real cost to someone else.

One important reason to keep track of these various hidden costs is because later on they may no longer be hidden. When indigenous teachers replace the "inexpensive" foreign teachers, or when the experiment in radio or television instruction succeeds so well that the schools need their own broadcast station, these real costs suddenly show up on the education budget. A good rule to remember is that no resources an educational system uses are truly free if they have a real economic value in some alternative use. Everything costs somebody something.

Hidden, nonbudgetary costs are especially crucial in many nonformal education programs that depend heavily on voluntary help and the use of borrowed facilities. These "free" resources have an economic value and their supply is limited.

Transfer Payments

The opposite of omitting an important cost is to count the same expenditure twice. This happens if you are not careful in dealing with so-called transfer payments. Broadly speaking, a transfer payment is simply a conveyance of purchasing power from one institutional or individual pocket to another, without any real expenditure taking place that would generate additional national product and income.

You should be especially alert for two particular possibilities. The first is where the national government makes educational subsidy payments, usually from the ministry of education's budget, to local governments or to private schools, which in turn spend the money on school buildings, teacher salaries, and other educational purposes. The payment from the ministry's budget is merely a cash transfer; it does not actually buy anything. It only

50

becomes a real expenditure when spent by the local government or the schools themselves. Thus take care not to count the same money twice when combining public and private or national and local educational expenditures.

The second possibility is the granting of student scholarships, fellowships, or bursaries that the students then spend on tuition fees, dormitory charges, and the like. The payment to the students is merely a transfer; the real expenditure occurs only when the students buy something with the money. Often, however, university budgets show both the transfer payment (under student assistance or some such label) and the costs of the educational services that the students partially pay for with the grants (for example, room and board, staff salaries). This is a legitimate (even if sometimes an illogical) accounting procedure for universities to use, but it can trap the unwary cost analyst into double counting.

Unit Cost of What Unit?

The term unit cost can also be a trap for the unwary. As noted in chapter 3, it is used most often to mean the recurrent annual cost per enrolled student, but a variety of other types of unit cost measures exist that are valuable for certain purposes, and keeping them straight is important. They include, for example,
• the average total cost per graduate
• the average capital cost per student place
• the average capital cost per occupied student place
• the average cost per teacher
• the average cost per classroom
• the average cost per school
• the average cost per course
• the average cost per square or cubic foot.

The most appropriate unit to use for costing depends on the particular item with which you are concerned. If you are costing the number of pencils and textbooks needed, or the food bill, then the individual student is the most appropriate unit because in these cases, cost varies in direct proportion to the number of students. If, however, you are estimating requirements for teachers, or for desks, maps, globes, and various other items of classroom equipment, then the classroom is usually the best unit, since the staffing and equipment requirements vary with the number of classrooms rather than with the number of students. When estimating heating and lighting costs, square or cubic footage may be the best unit.

To avoid confusion, when using the term unit cost, be explicit about what kind of unit is in question, unless this is already clear from the context.

Joint Costs

As the name implies, joint costs are common costs shared by a number of different educational units or activities. The teacher is a joint cost for all the students in a class; the principal and school secretary are joint costs for all the students in the school; maintenance of the building is a joint cost for the regular daytime and evening adult classes using it; and the ministry of education is a joint cost for all the schools in the system.

Difficulties often arise when you have to allocate joint costs to different users of the same service to calculate their respective total or unit costs. No standard solution is available for all cases. You simply have to devise the most reasonable basis you can in each instance, taking care not to use a more elaborate and time consuming method than the circumstances warrant, and being sure to apply consistently whatever formula you adopt.

The simplest method in many situations is simply to divide up the joint cost according to the number of students in each category affected, or by the number of classrooms or teachers or schools, as the case may be. We recommend that in disposing of joint cost problems, you content yourself with a pragmatic solution that seems reasonable and not get bogged down in metaphysical debates with your colleagues about, for example, how to divide school inspector costs between older teachers and younger teachers, or between first grade and fifth grade students.

When Do Costs Occur?

Another tricky problem is how to allocate costs by time periods. This problem arises mainly when dealing with capital costs, but it may also apply to research and development costs.

For illustration, take the case of a new university science building, built with a loan, which required three years to construct. While under construction, it tied up considerable capital that was yielding no return. Two questions immediately arise. First, to what year or years should this capital outlay and the interest charges be assigned for purposes of making a time series of capital expenditures? Second, in computing annual capital costs in subsequent years, how should you treat this building?

The best way to handle the first problem is to apportion the three-year capital outlay and interest charges between the three years of construction on the basis of actual cash disbursements in each year (if this information is available), since this gives the most accurate picture of what really happened. If you use this method, however, you should also follow it for all other capital outlays in your time series; otherwise the series will not be consistent and comparable from year to year. Alternative methods would be to assign the full amount of a new capital project either to the year of authorization, to the year when construction started, or to the year of completion. These solutions give a deceptive picture of actual capital outlays, but an accurate one of capital authorizations, construction starts, or completions. Decide which you want to show, and be sure to state clearly what method you have used or your readers may be misled.

The more important question is how to charge this new capital outlay against educational costs in the future. If you are computing the total cost per student (capital plus recurrent), charging the full capital costs to the first crop of students to use a new facility obviously makes no sense. The right approach would be to amortize the cost, including interest, over the building's estimated useful lifetime and apportion it annually to all the students who use it over time. We will return to the subject of amortization in chapter 6.

Research and Development Costs

These are the special costs involved in undertaking a new venture—such as a major experiment or innovation—that will become generally applied if successful. Research and development costs behave in special ways and present particular timing problems, similar to but more complicated than costs of a new building.

52

You must distinguish between the starting-up costs of such undertakings, which are one time only costs, and the longer-term "normal" costs that will occur later.

Generally, the cost per student during the initial phase of a major educational experiment or innovation is abnormally high. If you mistakenly view these costs as an indicator of future costs, the experiment might be thrown out on grounds of not being economically feasible. It is essential, therefore, to develop two sets of cost projections: the first applying to the developmental period; the second showing the anticipated normal costs beyond this period. This serves two important purposes: it prevents initial prejudice against the innovation; but it also guards against wishful thinking, for the projections may reveal that the longer-range normal costs, though lower than the initial costs, may still be too high for the experiment to be adopted generally. To take an extreme example, if may well be true that the children in a very poor country could learn more in computerized classrooms, but local officials have grave doubts whether the country can afford this new technology once the experimental period was over, regardless of how impressive the pedagogical results might be. "Appropriate" educational technologies are ones that not only fit the local situation pedagogically, but also fit the local pocketbook.

Next we turn to the important matter of trade-offs, in which you will inevitably find yourself heavily engaged.

Trade-Offs

If the world of educational systems was not one of limited resources (including time, the most fixed resource of all), there would be little need for cost analysis, but educational systems have always lived with limited resources and always will, even in the most affluent nations. Therefore the managers of educational systems are constantly having to choose between alternative ways of allocating and combining the resources available to get the best results.

What makes the choices so difficult is that they must simultaneously weight several sets of variables measured on quite different scales. It is not a simple matter, for example, of minimizing costs regardless of the educational consequences. Nor is it a simple matter of getting the best conceivable pedagogical results regardless of the cost. Rather, it is the much more complicated matter of striking a good balance between the pedagogical considerations on the one hand and the costs and other feasibility considerations on the other. This means that educational planners and decisionmakers constantly have to make trade-offs, and to do this well, they must again examine each situation through the lens of a systems analysis.

To bring the subject down to practical terms, let us take a few homely examples:

Example 1: A financial limit is imposed on a preliminary draft educational plan that had envisaged a large expansion of enrollments at all three education levels. Cost analysis reveals that with the limited additional funds available, 1,000 university students could be added, or 3,000 secondary students, or 15,000 elementary students, or some combination of all three within these financial limits. In this case, planners have to make a trade-off between the expansion of enrollments at different levels, which requires Solomon-like judgment. Cost analysis does not provide the answer, but it defines the limits within which the answer must fall.

Example 2: A classroom teacher devotes one hour each to reading, writing, and arithmetic every day, and the rest of the time to other subjects, recreation, and rest periods. The teacher is pleased with the class's progress on reading and writing, but perturbed by their slower progress in arithmetic. Should the teacher reallocate time, reducing the amount spent on reading and writing to improve arithmetic? Or should the teacher steal extra time for arithmetic from the other subjects, recreation, or rest periods? The costs here are in terms of time, not money, and the outputs are in terms of student learning results, health, and educational diversity. This is the sort of trade-off situation that confronts teachers all the time.

Example 3: A primary school, handicapped by resource scarcities and poor quality results, would like to add another teacher so as to reduce class size. It would also like to have substantially more textbooks and other self-instructional materials, but it does not have enough money to do both. The school is thus forced into a trade-off between adding the teacher or adding instructional materials. The question, of course, is which will improve learning results the most. Again cost analysis alone cannot decide the answer. It can only define the parameters of the choice so that the school administrators can make their decision on pedagogical grounds.

The business of trade-offs lies at the very heart of educational planning and decision making, basically because there is never enough time and resources available to do everything that might seem desirable. Educational planners must make choices, often very hard choices, because the decision to do more of one thing generally means doing less of something else. Educational systems often pay for a decision to expand enrollments rapidly by a decline in quality. Planners' responsibilities are not to make such choices themselves, but to see to it that the top administrators and politicians who have ultimate responsibility for decision making are well aware of what their trade-off options are, and the economic, pedagogical, and other important implications of each one.

5. Analyzing Recurrent Costs

Recurrent costs, as defined earlier, apply to human services and physical supplies that the educational process consumes within a single budget year. Since these typically amount to 80 percent or more of total educational costs, they merit major attention in any cost analysis, whatever its particular purpose.

Some General Guidelines

A few basic guidelines that apply to all types of recurrent costs in formal education follow. With appropriate modification, they are also relevant to nonformal education programs. Always bear in mind, however, that most nonformal education is inherently more quickly adaptable to needed changes than formal education, and that many nonformal programs receive few if any public funds and often make extensive use of contributed facilities and human services.

The Impact of Old and New Decisions

Although in economic theory, capital costs are *fixed* (in the short run) and recurrent costs are *variable,* as a practical matter, recurrent costs in education are also largely fixed in the short run and only acquire substantial variability as time goes one. This is because educational managers with a new budget that is, say, 10 percent higher than the previous year, actually have only limited room for maneuver in deploying these new funds. Most of the money is already committed as the result of previous decisions, contracts, and practices, some running back many years, such as old decisions on teacher salary structures and qualifications, staffing norms, and architectural designs. Generally, the managers must first satisfy these inherited commitments and the needs of on-going operations before they can consider any new ventures. If the educational managers still have as much as 5 percent of the new budget left for fresh expansion, improvements, special studies, and innovations, they can consider themselves lucky. This is especially true today, when budget reductions are more likely than annual increases.

If, however, the planners and managers take a longer view, five to ten years ahead, their margin for maneuver is much greater; and if they have clear objectives and priorities, and a well-conceived strategy, they can use this cumulative margin to achieve many important changes. This can only happen, however, if they examine every decision with care before it becomes cast in concrete. For in the same way that past decisions have imposed fixed commitments and constraints on the present, new decisions will have a binding effect on the future. A decision this year, for example, to eliminate primary school fees or to increase future retirement pensions will build higher recurrent costs into the budget for all future years and will be difficult if not impossible to reverse.

Projecting Future Costs

In assessing future recurrent costs, you should begin by examining present costs and recent trends, for these provide important clues to the future. To be sure, you cannot accurately estimate future costs simply by extrapolating past trends; you must allow for the influence of new policies and plans, prospective economic conditions, and a variety of internal and external cost-influencing forces that will make the future different from the past. Serious errors can result from assuming simplistically that major elements of recurrent costs will remain static. The real question is how fast and how far each of these elements is likely to travel in a given period, under various sets of dynamic assumptions.

If history is any guide, the chances are strong that your recurrent costs per student will rise in future years, and your main problem will be how to slow the rate of increase. If, however, your cost per student is actually standing still or even declining, the explanation is likely to be either (a) that quality is eroding (as the result of spreading resources thinner over more students), or (b) that you have instituted some effective cost-reducing measures compatible with preserving or improving quality.

To test your detective abilities, table 5-1 presents some figures from Nepal that show trends in enrollments and expenditure per student at each education level from 1973 to 1979. Note that the per student expenditure trends at all three levels reflect a curious reversal during this seven-year period. At both the primary and higher education level, cost per student rose substantially from 1973 to 1975 (a quite common phenomenon), but thereafter declined. At the secondary level, cost per student rose steadily from

Table 5-1. Nepal: Enrollments and per Student
Expenditure by Level, 1973-1979

Year	Total enrollment (number of students)			Per student expenditure (in current rupees)		
	Primary	Secondary	Higher	Primary	Secondary
1973	301,439	215,993	19,094	81.8	145.7	2,470
1974	401,034	221,583	21,760	93.3	157.7	3,070
1975	458,516	341,357	23,504	114.8	165.8	4,880
1976	643,835	262,748	21,047	100.4	190.7	4,060
1977	769,049	308,797	34,744	94.9	298.6	3,790
1978	875,494	370,231	31,942	100.9	183.0	3,677
1979	1,012,530	444,038	39,863	97.4	164.7	2,971

Source: Tribuhuvan University, Kathmandu, and ministry of education (from IIEP files).

1973 to 1977, but then declined rather sharply in 1978 and 1979. Make a list of all the possible explanations you can think of for this curious reversal of cost trends.

The Main Components of Recurrent Costs.

Recurrent costs include many different items, some very large, above all, teacher costs, and others relatively small, such as office supplies. A good general rule is to allocate your energies according to the relative quantitative importance of each item.

Another general rule is that the further you break down the costs into meaningful subdivisions, the more versatile, useful, and accurate your analysis will be. Thus, for example, separate unit cost figures for primary, secondary, and higher education obviously reveal more than a composite figure for all levels combined. Separate unit cost figures for rural and urban primary education, for secondary boarding and day schools, or for different university programs, will serve many more useful purposes, and all purposes more accurately, than broader averages for mixed categories.

This point is well illustrated by a recent IIEP study that compares the cost per student in secondary day schools and boarding schools in Morocco. The findings (see table 5-2) revealed that the boarding school cost was 2.7 times as high as day schools at lower secondary and 1.9 times as high at upper secondary.

Table 5-2. Morocco: Comparative Cost per Student for Secondary Day Schools and Boarding Schools, 1981 (in dirhams)

| Expenses | Lower secondary schools | | Upper secondary schools | |
	With boarding facilities	Without boarding facilities	With boarding facilities	Without boarding facilities
Day costs				
Teaching	1,083.44	1,083.44	2,327.33	2,327.33
School administration	216.63	248.58	260.86	310.06
Other costs	65.40	24.88	83.78	28.72
Sub-total	1,365.47	1,356.90	2,671.97	2,666.01
Boarding Costs				
Administration	1,053.77	dna	1,053.77	dna
Other expenses	1,222.29	dna	1,222.29	dna
Sub-total	2,276.06	dna	2,276.06	dna
Total	3,641.53	1,356.90	4,948.03	2,666.01
Ratio	2.68:1		1.86:1	

dna = does not apply
Source: M. Radi 1982.

Table 5.3. Classification of Recurrent Costs by Object and Purpose

| | ----------------------------Purpose---------------------------- | | | | |
Type of cost	Instruct-ion	Adminis-tration	Food & lodging	Transport-ation	General Main-tenance
1. Personnel costs					
a. Teachers					
b. Administrative staff					
c. Other staff					
2. Nonpersonnel costs					
a. Materials and supplies					
b. Utilities					
c. Miscellaneous					

To find out what is really happening, break down recurrent costs by object of expenditure (for example, teacher costs, other staff costs, and various nonpersonnel costs), and by purpose (for example, instruction, administration, student welfare services, transportation). You can summarize the results of such breakdowns on a cross-classification form similar to that in table 5-3 (using such categories and labels as fit your particular needs and conventions).

Whatever categories and estimating techniques you choose, apply them consistently so that your figures will be comparable among different institutions and from one year to the next. Be sure also to include all relevant costs, even if you must estimate some of them crudely. Finally, separating teacher costs from other staff costs and instructional costs from noninstructional costs is especially important because they vary in importance and tend to behave differently.

What Costs to Include and Exclude

Before you start compiling statistics of recurrent costs, be very clear about what it is you are trying to measure. For many purposes you will simply be measuring the financial costs of formal education to the public budget. Bear in mind when you do so, that this is an understatement of total educational costs to the economy. As noted earlier, it excludes all private costs, various hidden costs, and most of the costs of nonformal education (which may be substantial and may be critical to the nation's social and economic development). Remember also that it is not enough for you, as the planner or cost analyst, to know what your final figures include and exclude. You must label them clearly so that others can also know.

Nonteacher Recurrent Costs

This is a rather cumbersome label for what remains after you subtract teacher costs from total recurrent costs. Usually the main items included are other staff costs (including administrative and service personnel), instructional materials and supplies, other types of supplies and materials, maintenance and repairs, and scholarships and student welfare costs (for example, scholarships, transportation, school meals, boarding, health care).

The latter item—scholarships and student welfare—merits special attention because it is often surprisingly large in many developing countries at the secondary, and especially the postsecondary, levels (see table 5-4). In Tanzania it is also surprisingly large at the primary level. The high student welfare costs in higher education often include sizable fellowships for overseas study.

Table 5-4. Student Welfare Costs in Selected Developing Countries (around 1979/80)

Country	Percentage of total public recurrent costs	
	2nd level	3rd level
Algeria	9.4	46.3
Bangladesh	0.4	5.0
Burkina Faso	34.6	88.7
Congo	14.0	65.0
Cote d'Ivoire	34.2	52.2
Cuba	64.0	53.6
Malaysia	6.5	9.4
Nicaragua	4.5	91.0
Tanzania	32.8	43.9
Thailand	4.5	17.2
Tunisia	3.6	34.0

Note: Includes scholarships, transportation, subsidies for meals, dormitories, health services, and so on. These figures are not strictly comparable between countries because of differences in accounting practices.

Source: UNESCO 1983, table 4.4.

Another nonteacher cost, raw materials used by trainees in occupational training programs—such as wood, metal, or textiles—can also be sizable. When these are cut from the budget for "economy" reasons, as they often are, the cost-effectiveness of the program is likely to plummet.

A common practice in costing educational targets is to lump these nonteacher recurrent costs together and project them as a fixed percentage of teacher costs, using the present ratio of one to the other. This avoids having to make separate projections for each item of nonteacher recurrent costs. You can justify this "quick and dirty" method if you are simply making a fast preliminary check, for example, on the feasibility of alternative expansion targets. But for more accurate planning and decision making, this method can get you into serious trouble, for the following reasons. First, this crude method puts the entire burden for accuracy on your estimate of teacher costs, thus any error here, in either direction, becomes compounded. Second, the costs of nonteacher components often move differently from teacher costs; hence, to tie them rigidly together can lead to substantial error. A study of secondary school costs in the United Kingdom demonstrated the danger of assuming that nonteacher recurrent costs and teacher costs will maintain a fixed relationship from year to year. It showed, for example, that over a 13-year period, administrative staff and maintenance costs per student rose 46 percent, while teacher costs per student rose only 27 percent (all measured in constant prices). Third, if expenditures on teachers and on nonteacher items are seriously out of balance in the base period (as they frequently are in developing countries), this method tends to perpetuate the imbalance. Finally, as one moves upward from the primary school level, the ratio of nonteacher costs to teacher costs rises sharply (often moving from about 1 to 10 at the primary level to 1 to 1 at the university level). Thus substantial errors made in estimating nonteacher costs above the primary level can result in large errors in the final estimate of total costs.

To go beyond this crude method, however, requires substantial additional work. You must judge whether this is worthwhile case by case. It clearly was worthwhile, for example, in the case of the Morocco study (table 5-2) of secondary school costs that revealed major differences between costs per student in secondary day schools and boarding schools.

When you make separate projections for each major item of nonteacher cost, you must tie each estimate to an appropriate variable, such as the number of students, teachers, or classrooms. As mentioned earlier, the same variable will not do for all purposes. Requirements for textbooks, food, or student grants, for example, will vary mainly with the number of students, whereas utility and maintenance requirements will vary with the size and type of buildings; other items may vary with the number of teachers, classrooms, or administrative units.

Also as noted above, you must take particular care with scholarships and student welfare costs, such as transportation, school meals, board, and health services. Although these costs are basically tied to the number of students, they do not necessarily change uniformly with the overall number of students. For example, the proportion of secondary boarding students may decline over the years, thus reducing the relative size of boarding costs for secondary education as a whole. Or an elementary school system that has achieved high participation rates in urban areas and is now concentrating on raising rural school attendance, is likely to find its transportation and school lunch costs rising disproportionately. A large expansion of enrollments in higher education that raises the proportion of students from indigent families may cause a disproportionate increase in scholarship aid.

Differences in scholarship and student welfare costs help to explain the wide spread in average costs per student between primary education and higher levels. For example, for these to be less than 3 percent of recurrent costs in primary education but as much as 50 percent or more in higher education is not unusual (see table 5-4).

The Dynamics of Teacher Costs

The figures in table 5-5 underscore the dominant role played by teacher costs and how they vary from one education level to another. Here again the figures are drawn from widely scattered developing countries and are not strictly comparable because of the differences in accounting practices. For example, some combine administration costs with teachers costs, which causes the teacher/cost ratio to look somewhat higher than it really is. The African countries with very low teacher/cost ratios at the third level generally have limited higher education facilities of their own, hence the bulk of their third level expenditures goes into scholarships and welfare for students studying abroad. Nevertheless, the general picture portrayed by these figures is valid enough to make two basic points. First, teacher costs are a major portion of total recurrent costs in virtually all developing countries. Second, teacher costs frequently account for more than 90 percent of recurrent costs at the primary level, leaving little money for instructional materials and equipment, repairs and maintenance, or other essentials.

Teacher costs are constantly under the influence of dynamic forces operating both inside and outside the educational system. Virtually any change of educational policy affecting class size, programs, methods, or staffing patterns is likely to have an impact on teacher costs. Similarly, changes in supply-demand conditions for educated manpower in the economy at large are likely to have repercussions on teacher costs and on the size and quality of teacher supply. These realities again warn against making the simplistic assumption that the present average cost per teacher, or the teacher cost per student, will remain constant in the future.

We can demonstrate the point by looking at two features of every formal education system that have a major influence on the dynamics of teacher costs: the teacher salary structure and the composition of the teaching force.

Table 5-5. Teacher Emoluments as a Percentage of Total Public Recurrent Costs in Selected Developing Countries (around 1980)

Country	All levels combined (%)	First level (%)	Second level (%)	Third level (%)
Algeria*	64	98	83	28
Argentina*	87	92	90	82
Bangladesh	71	58	80	86
Bolivia	89	97	96	98
Burkina Faso*	61	99	64	10
Chile	84	88	98	79
Colombia	93	97	95	94
Congo*	71	99	84	17
Côte d'Ivoire	58	85	48	22
Ghana*	74	98	91	93
Guatemala	68	97	96	99
Honduras	88	94	62	96
Malaysia	69	91	74	90
Mexico	67	85	71	58
Republic of Korea	81	89	70	60
Syria	86	88	84	---
Thailand	80	91	86	60
Tunisia*	78	97	88	36
Venezuela	61	82	87	57
Zambia	63	89	38	74
Zimbabwe	80	83	82	100

* Includes administration.

Source: UNESCO 1983, table 4.4.

61

Although teacher salary structures in different countries differ in detail and terminology, they generally share four basic characteristics. First, each educational level has its own teacher classifications and salary schedules; the median salary is lowest for elementary teachers and highest for university professors, with secondary school salaries usually falling in between. Second, each education level has a hierarchy of classifications and salary schedules, based on professional qualifications. Different pay schedules may be in effect for men and women teachers, and for local and expatriate teachers. Some industrialized countries, such as the United States, have gradually abolished some of these distinctions and adopted a single salary schedule for elementary and secondary teachers and for men and women; but they still retain different pay scales according to professional qualifications and years of teaching service, and salaries in colleges and universities generally exceed those in primary and secondary schools. Third, each salary schedule contains incremental steps which each teacher climbs automatically, based on years of service, until reaching the ceiling. Fourth, teachers with lower qualifications can shift to a higher classification and salary schedule by improving their professional qualifications through in-service training.

The above characteristics are illustrated by Guinea's monthly salary schedule for primary and secondary school teachers in 1985, shown in table 5-6. Note that it ranges from 1,903 sylis per month for the lowest grade of teacher trainee (bottom of Class F scale) to 15,972 sylis per month for a principal of a higher secondary school (top of Class B). Note also the sizable biannual automatic increases based on years of services (averaging 4,932 sylis per year, for example, in the case of Class B teachers). The average salary per teacher and the overall teacher salary bill in any particular year will depend on the size of the teacher force and how it is distributed among the different classes and promotional steps.

The above types of salary differentials and automatic increments in pay endow teacher costs with an internal dynamism of their own. Even if the general level of teacher salaries remains stable, changes in the distribution and composition of the teacher corps from year to year can considerably alter the average cost per teacher at each education level and for the system as a whole. Some examples follow below.

• In a period when primary education is expanding much more rapidly than secondary and higher education, the average cost per teacher for the system as a whole tends to decline; but the reverse happens when expansion at the secondary and higher levels speeds up.

• If many young and poorly qualified teachers are hired during the first wave of an elementary school expansion, average cost per teacher at the elementary level declines; but later, as these young teachers grow older, and as many become upgraded through in-service training, the average cost per teacher will rise rapidly.

• As local teacher supplies improve, the substitution of indigenous teachers for foreign teachers raises the average cost per teacher if the foreign teachers were low-cost volunteers, but it lowers the average cost if the expatriates were high-cost, contract teacher.

In short, quite apart from what is happening to the overall size of the teacher corps or to pupil/teacher ratios (both of which obviously affect total teacher costs), changes in the composition of the teacher force have a strong influence on the average cost per teacher at each education level, thanks to

Table 5-6. Guinea: Monthly Salary Schedule for Primary and Secondary
Teachers by Category and Grade (1985) (in sylis)

Category and grade	Class B	Class C	Class D	Class E	Class F
Principal	15,972	9,801	6,413	5,192	4,301
1st grade					
3rd step	14,833	9,196	6,050	4,807	3,795
2nd step	13,893	8,591	5,808	4,554	3,421
1st step	13,068	7,986	5,566	4,301	3,036
2nd grade					
3rd step	12,100	7,502	5,324	4,048	2,783
2nd step	11,198	6,897	4,961	3,795	2,530
1st step	10,164	6,413	4,719	3,542	--
3rd grade					
3rd step	9,317	6,050	4,477	3,421	2,277
2nd step	8,833	5,808	4,114	3,289	2,156
1st step	8,228	5,566	3,872	3,036	2,024
Trainee	7,744	5,203	3,630	2,783	1,903
Average monthly increase per step	822	460	278	139	119
Average monthly increase per year of service	411	230	139	69	59
Average annual increase per year of service	4,932	2,760	1,668	828	--

-- = not applicable.

Note: Class A (not shown) is the highest and applies mainly to foreign teachers.
Classes B, C, D, E, and F relate to formal teacher qualifications, F being the least qualified. A beginning teacher in any category serves as a trainee for 3 or 4 years, or until
an opening is available, and thereafter automatically moves up one step with every
two years of additional service.

Source: UNESCO Education Department/Education and Finance Division.

the salary differentials and automatic increases embodied in the teacher
salary structure. In projecting teacher costs, therefore, you must pay close
attention to prospective changes in composition.

We must sound a special warning about the behavior of teacher costs in
an educational system that has been expanding rapidly for many years, but
then reduces its rate of expansion drastically, or even stops growing. This
is the situation in which most educational systems and institutions found
themselves in the 1980s. What happens in these circumstances, is that the
recruitment of young new teachers (at the bottom of the salary scale) is
sharply curtailed. Meanwhile the existing teaching staff grows steadily older, moves up the automatic salary escalator with increasing years of service,
and thus becomes increasingly costly (even in the absence of any general

salary increase). Unfortunately, this phenomenon is occurring at a time when educational systems everywhere are experiencing increasingly tight budgetary ceilings. Remember, therefore, to look closely at the prospective changes in store in the composition of the teaching (and also the administrative) staff in your particular educational system or institution. Getting the bad news early is better than discovering it too late to take remedial action.

Analyzing Recent Teacher Costs

The first requirement for making good projections of future teacher costs is to obtain a clear cross-sectional picture of the present teaching force and its costs, and a longitudinal picture of what has been happening to these in recent years. These pictures should reveal
* total teacher costs broken down by major subsystems,
* the relationship of teacher costs to total recurrent costs,
* the average cost per teacher at each level,
* the sources of finance for teacher costs,
* recent changes in the size and composition of the teaching force.
Outlined below are five simple exercises that will help you become acquainted with the techniques and problems involved in sketching the above pictures. You can probably obtain most of the data needed for these exercises from budgetary and teacher records in the national ministry of education and civil service directorate if your educational system is centralized. If it is decentralized, you may have to consult records at the state, district, or local level. The same basic approaches can be used for an individual institution, such as a university, or for a highly structured nonformal education program, such as an agricultural extension system.

To keep these exercises simple, they are confined to formal education and to teacher costs financed mainly by public funds. We have also left out any reference to expatriate teachers, but you may wish to include them as a separate category if they are important in your situation. Finally, if your system includes a number of part-time teachers, we suggest you convert them to full-time equivalent teachers for purposes of this analysis.

Exercise 1: Determining Total Teacher Costs

The aim of this exercise is to compile an overall picture of publicly financed teacher costs, broken down by education levels, for the most recent year for which reasonably complete data are available. Remember that teacher costs include more than salaries; ordinarily they include the following four components:
* *Salary payments to teachers.* These should be measured before income tax payments and should be segregated from overall personnel or staff costs, thereby excluding salaries and wages of administrators, clerks, custodial personnel, bus drivers, and so on.
* *Supplementary payments and allowances.* These include payments for overtime work, extra responsibilities, hardship posts, cost of living allowances, family allowances, and so on, which for all practical purposes are part of the teacher's take home pay. In some countries, these supplementary payments add up to substantial amounts. In Nepal, for example, the government provides an additional 50 to 110 percent of the basic pay for remote area allowances for nonlocal teachers working in remote districts.

Table 5-7. Publicly Financed Teacher Costs by Education Level and Type of Cost (1985)

Education level	Salaries	Supple-mentary payments	Benefits	Indirect costs	Sub-system totals
		Type of Cost			
Primary					
Secondary					
Postsecondary					
System total					

Note: Includes teachers in government and government-aided schools whose salaries and benefits are financed by public funds.

• *Special benefits*. These include retirement fund contributions, medical coverage, free housing, free tuition for children of teachers, holiday travel, and other fringe benefits of direct value to the teacher, but not part of take home pay.

• *Indirect teacher costs*. These include necessary costs of teacher recruitment or improvement that do not involve direct payments or benefits to teachers, such as the costs of recruiting trips and interviews, family moving costs, in-service professional improvement programs, and so on. These are usually only marginal in size and therefore can be estimated roughly.

The chances are that your public education budget accounts are not broken down into precisely these categories. In addition, certain costs, such as fringe benefits, may be carried partly on the budget of an agency other than the education ministry or department. All you can do in such cases is to use your best detective instincts and statistical ingenuity. Whatever solutions you arrive at for treating particular accounting problems, be sure to stick with them consistently and to leave clear tracks behind so that others will know exactly what you did. Finally, when you have summarized your findings in tabular form similar to that in table 5-7, be sure to give it an accurate descriptive heading and to include such qualifying footnotes as may be necessary to explain the figures. Incidentally, in countries that have quite different types of secondary schools, for example, general and vocational, and of postsecondary institutions, such as universities, teacher training colleges, and technical institutes, you must show them separately.

Exercise 2: Ratio of Teacher Costs to Total Recurrent Costs

With little additional effort, you can determine the relationship of teacher costs to total recurrent costs for the same year covered exercise 1, using the

Table 5.8. Ratio of Teacher Costs to Total Recurrent Costs (1985)

Education level	(1) Teacher costs	(2) Total recurrent costs	(3) Ratio of (1) to (2)
Primary			
Secondary			
Postsecondary			
System total			

Note: Covers only publicly financed costs in formal education institutions.

same sources of information. In arriving at the figures for total recurrent costs, be sure to exclude any items in the education budget that are not for formal education, such as the costs of museums, libraries, public recreation, special youth programs, and so forth. You can summarize your findings in a form similar to that in table 5-8.

Exercise 3: Average Cost Per Teacher

One further simple step will complete your sketch of present teacher costs, namely, the calculation of average recurrent cost per teacher. For this you will need to collect data on the number of teachers (full-time equivalent) at each education level for the same year as in the previous exercises, again including only teachers financed by public funds. By dividing the number of teachers at each level into the corresponding total teacher costs, you will arrive at a simple average cost per teacher for each level. This is only a crude average that, like most such averages, conceals important differentials; but when combined with similar figures for other years, it is a significant indicator of the general direction in which teacher costs are moving. At times it can be a crucial early warning signal of trouble ahead.

You can enter the results of exercise 3 on a summary table similar to that in table 5-9.

Exercise 4: Recent Trends in Teacher Costs

If you are still game, we recommend that you now repeat the three previous exercises for each of the five preceding years (though if you are hard pressed for time, you might limit yourself to only one earlier year, say five years back). Here again, if your system has different types of secondary and postsecondary institutions, you should show them separately. The exercise will be a worthwhile investment of your time because only in this way can you detect and measure the dynamic forces that have been altering educational costs in the recent past and that are likely to influence them in the future.

Table 5.9. Average Cost Per Teacher by Education Levels (1985)

Education Level	(1) Total recurrent costs	(2) Total teachers (full-time equiv.)	(3) Average cost per teacher (1) ÷ (2)
Primary			
Secondary			
Postsecondary			
System total			

Note: Includes only teachers in formal education financed by public funds.

The resulting time profile, presented in summary form as in table 5-10, may produce some surprises, even for education officials who have been closest to the situation. With luck, it will also provoke some searching questions as to why teacher costs have behaved in the manner shown.

Exercise 5: Sources of Finance for Teacher Costs

From the same basic data you assembled for the previous exercises, you can now put together an outline of where the funds to finance teacher costs came from in the same years. This will come in handy later when you are trying to determine what income is likely to be available to defray future teacher costs.

Remember to include all levels of government and to show their respective contributions separately. If the contributions were not specifically earmarked for teacher costs, but were available for recurrent costs generally, you can assume that a proportionate share went for teacher costs unless you have reason to believe otherwise.

Your findings, summarized on a form similar to table 5-11, will provide a view of teacher costs from the revenue side, as distinct from the expenditure side used in the earlier exercises. The totals should match your earlier tables.

The five exercises above will have given you both a snapshot and a moving picture of recent teacher costs in your educational system. This is the foundation necessary for projecting future costs and sources of finance, but the statistics alone are not enough. To benefit fully from the lessons of the recent past, you must determine why the statistics behaved as they did.

Table 5.10. Summary of Recent Trends in Teacher Costs (1980-85)

Education level	Year						Percentage increase 1980-85
	1980	1981	1982	1983	1984	1985	
Primary							
Total recurrent costs							
Total teacher costs							
Ratio of teacher costs to recurrent costs (%)							
No. of teachers [1]							
Average cost per teacher							
Secondary							
Total recurrent costs							
Total teacher costs							
Ratio of teacher costs to recurrent costs (%)							
No. of teachers [1]							
Average cost per teacher							
Postsecondary							
Total recurrent costs							
Total teacher costs							
Ratio of teacher costs to recurrent costs (%)							
No. of teachers [1]							
Average cost per teacher							
System total							
Total recurrent costs							
Total teacher costs							
Ratio of teacher costs to recurrent costs (%)							
No. of teachers [1]							
Average cost per teacher							

Note: Includes only teacher costs in formal education financed directly or indirectly by public funds.

1. Full-time equivalent.

Determining Why Teacher Costs Change

Discovering the causes of recent changes in teacher costs requires statistical ingenuity and some additional information. The changes were probably caused by a combination of several different factors. Your problem is to sort them out and measure their relative importance. The following exercise illustrates how you might go about this.

Let us assume that your exercise 4 (table 5-10) showed an increase of 55 percent in overall costs of secondary school teachers between 1980 and

Table 5-11. Sources of Public Funds for Teacher Costs (1980-85)

| | | | | Year | | | |
Education level	1980	1981	1982	1983	1984	1985
Primary teachers						
National government						
State government						
Local government						
Total						
Secondary teachers						
National government						
State government						
Local government						
Total						
Postsecondary teachers						
National government						
State government						
Local government						
Total						
System Total						
National government						
State government						
Local government						
Total						

1985. Theoretically, this could have been caused by an increase in the number of teachers, by an increase in the average cost per teacher, or by some combination of the two. Finding the answer is easy.

The data from which you constructed table 5-10 reveal, let us say, that the total number of secondary teachers increased from 5,000 in 1980 to 6,300 in 1985—an increase of 26 percent. This is obviously a good part of the explanation, but it is not all of it. Table 5-10 also tells you that the average cost per secondary teacher rose about 15 percent in the same period. On the face of it, this would seem to be the rest of the answer. However, we still need an explanation of why the average cost per teacher rose by this amount.

An 11 percent across the board salary increase granted to all teachers in this period is part of the explanation, but what about the remaining 4 percent? Logically, this can only be explained by a change in the composition of the teacher force. A quick check confirms this. Going behind your teacher totals, you find that the number of Grade A teachers (with higher salaries) increased from 2,000 to 3,000, while Grade B teachers increased only from 3,000 to 3,300. Thus, the qualifications profile of the teacher force improved, and this would seem to account for the missing 4 percent.

But wait. The answer is not that simple. By examining the composition of the teacher force more closely, you discover that important changes have taken place in the distribution of teachers by points on the promotional steps of the salary scale. To see this clearly we need another table, table 5-12. This table shows a salary range for Grade A teachers from a minimum of US$1,000 to a maximum of US$2,200, and for Grade B teachers from US$500 to US$1,400; but the table also seems paradoxical.

Table 5-12. Illustration: Changes in the Distribution of Teachers on the Automatic Salary Promotion Scale

| Steps on salary scale | Number of teachers at each step 1980 | | 1985 | |
	Grade A	Grade B	Grade A	Grade B
2,200	300		300	
2,000	200		200	
1,800	200		300	
1,600	250		400	
1,400	300	450	500	700
1,200	350	250	600	600
1,000	400	300	700	500
900		300		500
800		350		400
700		400		300
600		450		300
500		500		
Average salary (US$)	1,530	860	1,453	1,018

Note: The salaries shown were those prevailing in 1980, prior to the across the board increase of 11 percent. Since this increase applied uniformly to all points on all salary scales, we can ignore it for present purposes.

We know that the number of Grade A teachers (average salary of US$1,530 in 1980) increased 50 percent from 1980 to 1985, whereas the number of Grade B teachers (average salary of US$860 in 1980) increased by only 10 percent. Then should the overall average cost per teacher not have increased much more than 4 percent? Yes, indeed, it should have. In that case, a strong cost reducing force that we have not yet accounted for must have been at work.

The mystery is quickly solved. As you can see from the figures in table 5-12, the average salary for Grade A teachers declined by 5 percent over the five years (from US$1,530 to US$1,453), whereas the average for Grade B teachers rose by about 18 percent (from US$860 to US$1,018). This was caused by the redistribution of teachers by salary steps. Many new Grade A teachers came in at the bottom of the Grade A salary scale, while the number at the bottom of the Grade B scale declined and the number at the top increased. In other words, the Grade A teacher group grew younger, while the Grade B group grew older. This would occur partly through recruitment of new teachers, partly through wastage due to death, retirement

70

or simple dropping out, and partly from the progression of teachers through successive grades on the salary scale.

To summarize, the 55 percent increase in total teacher costs resulted from
  • a 40 percent increase in the number of teachers,
  • an 11 percent salary increase for all teachers,
  • a 4 percent net increase in the average cost per teacher,
resulting from a combination of (a) an increase in the proportion of Grade A teachers, and (b) a redistribution of teachers by salary steps.

The first two cost increasing factors (a rise in the number of teachers and in the general level of teacher salaries) were fairly easy to identify and measure; but the third factor (changes in composition of the teaching force) was more subtle and required more effort to detect and measure. This example demonstrates why when you are projecting future teacher costs, looking carefully at any likely changes in the composition of the teacher force, as well as at changes in its size and in the general level of teacher salaries is important. Otherwise you may be tricked into a serious error. For example, looking back at the figures in table 5-12, we can see that by 1990, the large number of new teachers at the low end of the Grade A scale in 1985 will have moved up the automatic promotion scale, causing the average salary of Grade A teachers to turn upward (unless they are offset in the meantime by a large number of new teachers coming in at the bottom).

Projecting Future Teacher Costs

Knowing how teacher costs have behaved in the recent past, you are now much better equipped to forecast their future behavior. But your work is only half done. Remembering the earlier point about the many internal and external factors that influence teacher costs, you must now consider carefully how each of these factors may influence teacher costs in the future. You will need to pay special attention to the following items:
  1. teacher requirements;
  2. teacher supply prospects;
  3. changes in the composition of the teaching force;
  4. changes in the general level of teacher salaries;
  5. price inflation;
  6. changes in the general structure of salary and wage relationships in the economy;
  7. teacher training costs; and
  8. expatriate teachers.

Projecting Teacher Requirements
We cannot examine methodologies to project student enrollments and teacher requirements here, but we emphasize that unless these projections are solidly prepared, you cannot make trustworthy projections of teacher costs.

The most commonly used method to calculate teacher requirements is simply to apply the present pupil/teacher ratio (or any desired modification of it), to the projected number of students at each education level for the final year of the plan period. The resulting figure shows the number of teachers needed to serve the projected number of students, and by how much the present number must be enlarged. You can then calculate the total

71

cost of teachers in the final plan year by applying an appropriate figure of average cost per teacher at each education level (either the present average cost or, more likely, some modification of it).

This simple method is handy for making a quick, rough check of feasibility, but its deficiencies are too great to make it a reliable tool for careful planning. First, it tells you nothing about the other years in the plan period, or about the number of new teachers that will be needed to replace those in the present stock who will retire, die, or resign. It only tells you the net addition to stock required, which is not an adequate guide for planning teacher supply. Second, applying a single pupil/teacher ratio, for example, to all primary education in the nation, obscures important differentials that may affect the real demand for teachers in the next five years, such as the differences in the pupil/teacher ratio and class size between urban and rural schools. In reality, many existing classes may be undersized and capable of absorbing increased enrollments with no corresponding increase of teachers; whereas in other situations, oversized classes may need to be reduced, whether or not enrollments expand.

You will get a much more reliable estimate of teacher requirements, therefore, by basing it on the number of classes that need to be staffed, not on the number of students. When you estimate the additional number of classes needed, you should differentiate between (1) urban classes, of which the country may need more, both to reduce currently oversized classes and to handle a net increase in students; (2) rural classes in existing schools that can probably absorb more students; and (3) classes in new rural schools, built to serve new areas, that will obviously need new teachers.

For all the reasons given, we urge you to look skeptically at any teacher requirement figures before accepting them as a sound basis on which to calculate future teacher costs.

Projecting Teacher Supplies

Regardless of how carefully you calculate teacher requirements, they can turn out to be wide of the mark if you do not test them for feasibility against teacher supply prospects. An educational system may theoretically need a given increase in teacher stock to accommodate more students, but if you have clear evidence that a physical shortage of new teachers will make it impossible to recruit this number, then adjusting the projected requirements to fit the likely supply is more realistic and responsible. Otherwise, you will end up costing teachers who will not be there. At the same time, you may fail to allow sufficient financing to expand teacher training capacity and output to reduce the teacher shortage.

Projecting the Composition of the Teaching Force

The foregoing approaches to estimate future teacher requirements, adjusted to fit the realistic supply prospects, will give you a more accurate estimate of the number of teachers to be financed, but the problem of projecting the composition of the teacher stock still remains.

In addition to what we have already said about this matter, we suggest the following practical method if you do not have good data on the present distribution of teachers by years of service and steps on the promotional scale, but you do have data on past teacher training output and on the present distribution of teachers by professional categories. In this situation, which is quite common, you can use a trial and error method to arrive at an estimated distribution of teachers by points on the salary scale. It consists of breaking down the present stock of teachers on the basis of past annual graduating classes from teacher training institutions who entered teaching the following year. You then calculate how far up the automatic promotion ladder each group of graduates should be in the present year, allowing arbitrarily for some assumed rate of attrition. This rate varies considerably from country to country, and within each country according to the status accorded teachers, the conditions of service, and the structure of the teaching force. Two percent would be a low annual attrition rate, 4 percent a high one. You perform the same exercise for each professional category of teachers coming from different training programs. The result gives you a theoretical distribution of teachers in the present stock by years of service and position on the promotion scale. To test it out, you can then cost the present teacher force, assuming this distribution, on the basis of the existing salary schedule. If the resulting total teacher bill differs substantially from the actual bill, you can then make successive adjustments in the theoretical distribution pattern until its total cost coincides with the actual total shown in the budget accounts. You can then use this adjusted theoretical pattern to project future changes in the composition of the teaching force.

Projecting Teacher Salaries

Having projected the size and composition of the future teacher force, you still have to put a price on the package. One way is simply to cost it at existing teacher salary rates. If, however, local conditions suggest that one or more general teacher salary increases are likely in the next few years, you must take this into account. Since you cannot be sure, the best practice is to make two or three alternative assumptions and cost each one out.

You should distinguish between two possibilities: first, when a country is experiencing a general price inflation and teacher salaries may be changing in relation to the cost of living, and second, when the relationship between teacher salaries and the general structure of wages and per capita income in the economy is changing. Either phenomenon can affect not only teacher costs, but education's ability to attract and retain an adequate supply of teachers.

Allowing for Inflation

The exercises suggested earlier in this chapter dealt with teacher costs in terms of current prices and salaries prevailing in each particular year; but as we have seen, current prices can be deceptive if the economy is undergoing substantial price inflation. If, for example, teachers are granted a 10 percent across the board salary increase in a given year, but the cost of living index rises 20 percent in the next 12 months, the teachers clearly end up worse off than before their salary increase. Their real income, measured in constant prices and real purchasing power, has declined.

The experience of primary school teachers in Honduras shows vividly what inflation can do to the real income of teachers. As table 5-13 shows, the basic salary of primary teachers stood still from 1970 to 1978, while prices rose 80 percent. Between 1979 and 1984, teacher salaries kept pace with inflation. They increased 62.5 percent against price increases of 57 percent, but they never recovered the ground lost between 1970 and 1978.

Inflation has also seriously victimized teacher salaries and overall education budgets in a great many other countries in recent years. In some

73

Table 5-13. Honduras: Index of Basic Salary of Primary School Teachers

Year	Salary Index	Price Index
1970	100.0	100.0
1975	100.0	138.3
1977	100.0	163.8
1978	100.0	180.3
1979	130.0	192.7
1980	145.0	214.1
1981	150.0	226.6
1982	150.0	244.0
1983	150.0	262.8
1984	162.5	290.4 (estimate)

Source: UNESCO, Education Department Education and Finance Division, unpublished files.

countries, strong teachers' unions have succeeded in negotiating automatic salary adjustments tied to annual cost of living increases. This is an understandable protective measure for any organized employee group exposed to inflation. Yet ironically, if widely adopted throughout the economy, such automatic escalator provisions could simply fuel an already spiraling inflation—unless it finally forces the government to adopt much more stringent anti-inflationary fiscal and monetary policies, such as heavier taxes on wages and salaries, the reduction or elimination of consumer subsidies on food, housing, and other items, and even the freezing of prices and wages.

If you live in an inflation-prone country, we suggest that you establish, with the help of a local economist, a weighted index of teacher remuneration. Since the data on teachers' salaries should be readily available within the ministry of education, this would be a relatively easy task. You can regularly compare this to the cost of living index. It will be useful both to project teacher costs and to weigh alternative salary policies.

We also suggest again that you make alternative assumptions about the future rate of inflation. In all probability, your government will not consider it prudent to publish those assumptions lest they become self-fulfilling prophecies and political liabilities. Therefore you may decide to label your contingency projections "unofficial" and keep them locked away. The hard truth is, however, that where rampant inflation has been going on for some years, the greatest victory the government can hope for is to slow it down substantially, not to stop it altogether. Therefore, simply assuming that prices and salaries would suddenly become stabilized could mislead decisionmakers seriously. Less ideal prospects must be frankly contemplated if educational planning is to be part of the real world.

Foreshadowing Changes in Wage Relationships

Apart from inflation, teachers' relative income and the cost of teachers to the educational system may rise, fall, or remain steady, depending on how teachers' salaries behave relative to average per capita income and to other wages and salaries in the economy. A number of possibilities exist, and your problem is to choose some assumptions that best fit your particular economy's conditions and prospects.

74

One commonly used assumption is that the real incomes of teachers will move up (or down) in line with incomes generally in the country. Thus, for example, if real income per capita for the nation at large is expected to rise by 2 percent each year, thanks to economic growth and rising productivity in the economy as a whole, then your projection of teacher costs might allow for an average rise of 2 percent each year in the real salaries of teachers (whether or not the productivity of teachers rises by this amount). This was a reasonable assumption to make in the 1960s and early 1970s in the case of countries with relatively full employment and a tight supply-demand balance for educated manpower; but in times of sizable unemployment among graduates, as in the 1980s, it could be an unrealistic assumption to make.

An alternative assumption, also commonly used, is that the real salaries of teachers (adjusted for inflation) will remain constant. This is tantamount to saying either (a) that per capita incomes as a whole will remain constant (possibly because population is growing at the same rate as the economy), and teacher salaries will retain a constant relationship to average per capita income and to other wages and salaries, or (b) that teachers as a group will not participate in the productivity gains of the economy—in other words, their real earnings will stand still even though the earnings of other groups rise.

The third possibility, of course, is to assume that teachers' real earnings will rise faster than the incomes of others, placing teachers in the favored position of getting a disproportionate share of the economy's gains. This would be the case, for example, if teacher salaries (after adjusting for any changes in consumer prices) rose 5 percent annually, while per capita earnings of employed persons in general rose an average of only 2 percent annually. Finding examples of anywhere this has actually happened in recent years is difficult, however. In many countries, just the opposite has occurred; teacher salaries have lagged behind other wage categories.

In any event, what happens to teachers' salaries relative to other salaries and job opportunities in the economy is bound to affect the education system's ability to attract and retain good teachers. Similarly, what happens to the supply of potential teachers relative to the number of unfilled teaching positions available will affect the quality of teachers the education system can recruit at its prevailing salary levels.

In these respects, the situation in most countries has now changed greatly since the halcyon days of the 1960s and early 1970s when educated manpower was in short supply and heavy demand. In countries with currently high and rising unemployment among new graduates, and with the number of openings for new teachers contracting, the education system should in theory (other things being equal) be able to recruit better quality people at its prevailing salary levels. The trouble is that other things do not remain equal. For example, if teacher salaries continue to lag behind inflation and behind wages in comparable types of employment, if overcrowded classrooms become even more overcrowded, and if the schools become increasingly bureaucratized, then a teaching career becomes steadily less attractive, thereby putting able young graduates off teaching and also prompting the ablest present teachers to look for other jobs.

This is precisely the dilemma that so many financially hard pressed school systems in developing countries are facing today. With their budgets no longer growing as they did earlier (or even contracting in real terms), yet with the pressures to keep expanding still as strong as ever, they find it extremely difficult even to sustain the present real level of teacher salaries, much less improve them.

Thus educational planners and cost analysts everywhere, in close consultation with knowledgeable local economists, should choose a reasonable set of assumptions about what is likely to happen to teachers' salaries and the teacher supply in the coming plan period. In so doing they should bear in mind that teacher costs and teacher supply live in a highly dynamic world, and to project them reasonably accurately, the planners' assumptions must be equally dynamic. In addition, finding ways to improve the productivity of teachers and the internal efficiency of education systems is vital. Without such improvements, the dilemma just described is unlikely to be resolved.

The Costs of Teacher Training

In the exercises earlier in this chapter, we omitted the costs of teacher training in the interest of simplicity, but now we must consider them for they have a substantial direct and indirect bearing on teacher costs.

Logically, teacher training costs fall in the category of capital costs as they involve expenditures in one time period that are intended to result in useful services in later periods. However, customary accounting practice does not treat them as capital costs except where new physical facilities for teacher training are involved. We strongly recommend that you not blend teacher training costs with recurrent costs for present classroom services; treat them in a separate category so that they can be clearly related to future teacher supplies and costs. This applies to both preservice and in-service training.

In any one year, teacher training costs are likely to be a modest fraction of total education costs, but do not be deceived by this. During a period of rapid expansion, they can add up to a substantial total over a few years. More important, they can also have a large multiplier effect on future teacher costs, not only by adding to the number of trained teachers, but by raising the average level of teacher qualifications.

One of the strategic uses of cost analysis is to assess alternative approaches to teacher training and choose the one that is both pedagogically sound and most economically affordable. A further important strategic use is to help policymakers decide how best to allocate scarce resources between preservice training of new teachers and in-service training aimed at refreshing and up-grading the existing teaching staff. Both the relative costs and relative time factors, as well as pedagogical considerations, play a major role in such decisions. If a country puts all its effort into preservice training, it will take many years to make a sizable impact on the quality of the whole teacher force; but if it follows the reverse course of putting all the resources into in-service training, the vicious circle of poor quality new teachers may never be broken. Thus countries have to strike the best balance.

Analysis of teacher training costs becomes critical when planning and appraising any major innovation or educational reform that will require retraining many existing teachers and overhauling the preservice training of new teachers, both of which carry sizable cost implications. Successful implementation of many a promising innovation or reform (on paper) has failed precisely because the teachers—the ultimate implementers—were never adequately trained in how to make it work.

76

An important question to ask about any program of preservice teacher training is: How much does it cost to put a newly trained teacher in a classroom? Often it costs much more than meets the eye. Heavy wastage of trainees during the training period, plus heavy attrition among successful graduates who finally choose employment other than teaching, can put the cost of each graduate that does enter teaching at a high multiple of the average annual cost per student enrolled in teacher training institutions. The cost jumps even higher if many of the newly trained teachers fail to remain in teaching very long. If a teacher remains for 30 years, his or her original training cost, amortized over the whole period, is obviously much smaller than if the new teacher remained for only 2 or 3 years. Thus when dealing with teacher training costs you must get the best data you can on three different rates of attrition: (1) dropouts from teachers training; (2) teacher training graduates who fail to enter teaching; and (3) graduates who enter teaching but depart prematurely. You should also consider a fourth factor, a kind of "negative attrition", that is, teachers who return to the profession after leaving.

The most important question of all to ask about teacher training costs is this: What impact will a given program or strategy of teacher training (either preservice or in-service) have on future recurrent costs of teachers by altering the qualifications structure of the teaching force? This is an extremely crucial question for any developing country that has a large proportion of unqualified teachers and is anxious to reduce this proportion drastically within the next few years. As part of the strategy, the country may secure sizable external assistance to replace its small and inadequate teacher training institutions with larger and "more modern" ones modeled after the best ones in some donor country. Enthusiasm rides high until some hard-nosed cost analyst examines all the cost implications of the proposed strategy, including not only the much higher future cost of producing the "new type" teachers but, even more important, the enormous impact this rapid up-grading strategy will have on future recurrent costs for teachers. The shocking conclusion may be that the proposed strategy—unless it is stretched over a much longer period—will lead the education system straight into bankruptcy. This is not just a hypothetical scenario; something similar happened several years ago in one African country, which narrowly escaped plunging blindly ahead with just such a financially disastrous strategy.

Expatriate Teachers

This matter affects only a limited number of nations, mostly in Africa, but for them it is exceedingly important.

Two basic points are vital. First, the cost of expatriate teachers usually differs greatly from the cost of equivalent local teachers. It is usually much higher when they are foreign "contract teachers" who receive all their salary and allowances, as well as transportation, from the host nation. Even when a substantial foreign subsidy is involved, the local costs may be higher than for an indigenous teacher. In some instances, for example, the allowances to expatriate teachers for housing alone has cost more than the total salary of local teachers with equivalent qualifications. Volunteer teachers, however, may cost considerably less to the host country than equivalent local teachers. Thus when projecting future teacher costs, you must estimate carefully the number and types of expatriate teachers and how they are financed, for this can make a large difference to total teacher costs.

77

The second point is that expatriate teachers are a highly volatile component of the total teaching corps. Not only do they remain for relatively short periods—typically one or two years—but their percentage of the whole teaching staff keeps shifting. Understandably, African countries are eager to Africanize their teaching staff as rapidly as possible, and indeed, many have made great progress, but the rate at which they do this depends (a) on how fast they can build up their own teacher supply, and (b) on how rapidly they are attempting to expand their educational system, particularly in secondary and higher education where foreign teachers are most needed. A relatively small marginal increase in the rate of expansion can result in a large proportionate increase in the number of expatriate teachers needed.

6. Analyzing Capital Costs

When capital costs are spread over a period of years, they typically account for a modest fraction of the total unit cost per student. Nevertheless, they deserve the careful attention of planners and cost analysts for several reasons.

• Capital outlays usually involve large, lump sum expenditures, which raises special financing problems. Borrowed capital funds must later be paid back with interest, thus mortgaging future revenues for years to come.

• Apart from debt service, the creation of additional facilities increases future operating costs; the recurrent costs of using and maintaining a new educational facility can readily equal the initial capital cost during each subsequent five-year period.

• The design of new facilities can impose severe constraints on altering educational technologies and teaching practices in the years ahead, thereby inhibiting needed changes and innovations and perpetuating old inefficiencies.

• The planning of new facilities provides a strategic occasion for making full use of both existing and future facilities, which is a major key to improving overall educational efficiency and holding down costs.

• The creation of new facilities for new programs in any one sector of the educational system can have major repercussions, including cost and revenue impacts, on other sectors. Unless these are identified, assessed, and provided for in advance, the new program may later create severe difficulties elsewhere and encounter setbacks.

Some Illustrative Parables

A few parables about building schools, all of which have actually occurred, will demonstrate the importance of using foresight in planning new educational facilities.

Parable One: A Tale of False Economy

School authorities in a certain community decided to substitute lower-cost roofing, siding, and flooring materials in their new school to cut costs. The savings released funds for a much needed playing field and everyone was pleased—until it turned out that the savings were false. A few years after the new school was opened, the extra costs of janitorial services, frequent repainting and repairs, not to mention replacing the storm-torn roof, added up to five times the "savings."

The moral of this particular parable is that a penny saved in building a school is not always a penny earned; it is sometimes the cause of losing more pennies later.

Parable Two: The School That Was Too Well Built

Having learned their lesson, the same school authorities built their next school of the best materials, rugged enough to outlast their grandchildren. Its floors and walls were thick, solid, and soundproof. All surfaces cleaned easily and never needed repainting or repair. The roof could withstand any storm. It was more expensive, of course, but authorities expected to recoup the extra costs many times over by later savings on custodial and maintenance costs. Indeed, to the great relief of each year's operating budget, this is what happened. Once more, everyone was pleased—until one day the unexpected happened.

Research studies based on a wide range of experiments in other school systems convinced the school authorities that their pupils would learn much more at little or no extra cost if they adopted certain innovations, including team teaching and instructional television combined with self-instructional programmed materials. An exciting new world of learning opened before their eyes, until they suddenly realized that their solid new school was a handicap. Its traditional, cell-like classrooms, built to accommodate 30 students and a teacher using 19th century pedagogical methods, prevented the flexible redeployment of space and people that was required to take full advantage of these promising innovations.

Reluctantly, the authorities adopted a compromise solution. They would adapt the new technologies to the building, not the building to the new technologies, which would reduce their effectiveness considerably. And since they did cost something extra, it was doubtful that, on balance, the school's cost-effectiveness had been improved.

The moral is that old-fashioned buildings can prevent progress; school authorities should plan new educational facilities flexibly so as to accommodate whatever new and better technologies may come along, perhaps even before the new school is finished.

Parable Three: The Right School in the Wrong Place [1]

School authorities in a newly independent nation concluded that their colonial type of academic secondary school was obsolete and irrelevant to local needs. Hence they launched an experiment involving a new type of multipurpose school that combined vocational training and university preparation. Careful pedagogical planning went into the project and enthusiasm ran high; if the new model succeeded, it would light a new way for the whole system.

Unfortunately, it did not succeed. It failed miserably and set the country's educational progress back several years. It was not because the pedagogical planning was unsound or the resources inadequate. Basically it was

---

[1]   IIEP has published some useful methods that planners can use to locate schools in the right places. See the selected reading list at the end of this book.

because this "lighthouse" school, for quite accidental political reasons, was located in a remote area where students could not get to it easily and where its light could not be seen by other educators. For some years, its enrollments ran well below capacity, causing its operating costs per student to be inordinately high. To remedy this situation, the authorities added expensive boarding facilities. This remedy worked, the school became full, but now its costs per student ran even higher because of the room and board costs. By now, unfortunately, disenchantment with the whole idea of multipurpose secondary schools had spread throughout the country—mostly for the wrong reasons—and the classical academic high school continued to be the national model, despite the generally acknowledged fact that it was a misfit.

The obvious moral is that new schools should be located for the convenience of students and teachers, not politicians. Educational planners can help in this matter by demonstrating clearly the comparative costs, convenience, and pedagogical advantages of alternative locations so clearly that politicians will appreciate the risks they run by insisting that a costly school be put in an irrational location.

Parable Four: The Strange Case of Too Many Schools

A poor nation with a dispersed rural population finally achieved its cherished goal of universal primary education, only to be disappointed. The costs were high and kept mounting, yet the educational results were notoriously poor. Close analysis showed why: paradoxically, the nation had built too many schools.

The country had continued the traditional custom of a school for each village. Meanwhile, many villagers had moved to the cities and there were too few students to fill the classrooms of the rural schools. The result was a low pupil/teacher ratio and abnormally high costs per student compared to urban schools, yet poorer learning results because the best teachers preferred to work in the cities, where they had better equipment, a richer curriculum, and the company of other teachers.

In due course, the government adopted a plan to abolish the small, traditional schools over a period of years as older teachers and school buildings reached retirement age, and to replace them with new medium-sized schools that served groups of neighboring villages. This added some new transportation costs, but they were offset by the lower instructional costs per student in normal-sized classes. More important, the teachers preferred these larger schools; so did the students, and they learned more. Naturally, local opposition to the school consolidation was considerable initially—no village likes to lose its school. Soon, however, the satisfaction of parents and children with the superior performance of the new schools lessened the opposition, and the lower unit costs pleased the taxpayers. The government took these lessons into account as it planned an expansion of secondary education.

The moral of this story is that the nostalgia that adults often feel for the one-room village school can impose heavy penalties on their children's education and on the public purse. A prerequisite for being able to afford good schools and universities is that they be of at least the minimum size that is economically and pedagogically viable. Yet in some cases, due to the very large dispersion of populations in some regions, small, one-teacher schools are the only solution that could be reasonably considered.

Parable Five: An Educational White Elephant

A handsome, new, foreign assisted, technical school in a developing country was dedicated jointly by the prime minister and the foreign ambassador with great hope and enthusiasm. Sad to say, it soon became an embarrassment to both. The reasons, in retrospect, were obvious.

The ambassador's nation, in all good faith, had met its promise to deliver a fine, new technical school, with equipment as modern as the best at home. To be sure, it had cost more than expected because the policy of "tied aid," which the ambassador's country insisted on, had required that many of the materials, virtually all the equipment, and much of the expert manpower be imported from back home. This cost a great deal more than if the recipient country had been given the money outright and allowed to build the school in its own way. This was all in the past, however. The real problem and the cause of the embarrassment was the high running cost, which the recipient nation had to shoulder and could ill afford.

No one had looked into the running costs very seriously; officials had been too preoccupied with the initial capital costs. Also, they had paid too little attention to the practical problems of recruiting, training, and paying local technical teachers, of which there were virtually none. Not surprisingly, much new equipment stood around in crates, unused, while other equipment soon broke down for lack of proper care and maintenance, all because of the lack of trained personnel. Most troublesome of all, local employers complained that the graduates of this new technical school did not fit their needs; they were overtrained or mistrained for local types of work, and they came on the job with inflated expectations of becoming shop supervisors overnight.

The moral of this sad parable is that educational gifts sometimes turn into white elephants that can devour the budgets of poor educational systems. The best way to avoid a white elephant is to discover its costly feeding habits in ample time to avoid getting stuck with it. With a modicum of tact and diplomacy, a country should be able to obtain instead a hard working elephant with a good disposition and a more moderate appetite, who fits into the local scene more comfortably.

Parable Six: The Accordion Schools That Saved Money

A developing country's educational planners, helped by demographers and manpower economists, plotted the changes likely to occur in the student population over the next decade by age and geographic distribution, as well as by likely changes in the economy's employment patterns. Their analysis showed that certain currently pressing educational and manpower demands could be expected to subside after a few years, while other types could be expected to increase. For example, once the large backlog of demand for primary education in various urban neighborhoods was met, demand would stabilize at a lower level. Meanwhile, migration from particular rural areas would diminish educational demand there, but would correspondingly raise the demand in certain urban areas. The planners could foresee similar ups and downs in the demand for various types of technical and professional training, not least of all for teacher training.

Thus, the planners realized that if they planned educational capacity simply to fit today's pattern of demand, it would be unsuitable for tomorrow's pattern. The result would be unused capacity in some places, and not enough in others. To avert such costly misinvestments, the country adopted a new and imaginative strategy of educational expansion. It was based on a distinction between permanent demand and temporary demand, and a corresponding distinction between permanent capacity and temporary capacity. To illustrate: projections showed a need for 1,000 new secondary teachers per year during the next five years to meet present deficits and expansion requirements. After that, requirements would decline steadily to only 400 new teachers per year to meet replacement needs and to support a slower expansion rate. Hence, the permanent demand would be for about 400 new teachers a year, but for the time being, there was an additional temporary demand of 600 per year.

The strategy had two thrusts. One was to provide lasting solutions for permanent needs and cheaper solutions for temporary needs. Thus, for example, the construction of new teacher training facilities would be limited to an output capacity of only 400 teachers per year, while provisional and less satisfactory quarters, such as old army barracks or estate houses, were adapted, and borrowed professors were used to train an additional 600 teachers to meet the peak demand.

The strategy's thrust involved the "accordion principle." In neighborhoods where planners expected demand for primary and secondary education to grow steadily over the years, new "modular" schools were built to which additional modules could be added later. This required buying and developing larger sites than were needed in the short run, but avoided the premature construction of school space. Over the years, this would save on capital costs. Conversely, in areas where planners expected the school population to decline, they installed demountable classrooms. These were sturdy, prefabricated structures, also modular in design, that could be moved by trailer from surplus to deficit areas.

The initial efforts to design and develop the demountable units ran into a variety of technical problems, but once they were overcome and factory production got underway, the cost per classroom, including moving, fell below the cost of a regular classroom. Needless to say, many people, including many educators, at first opposed the idea of standardized, demountable schools, considering them somehow dehumanizing and unaesthetic. But they relented as the units proved themselves to be educationally efficient, and demonstrated that each school could have a distinctive personality. The modular units could be arranged differently to fit the contours and conditions of each site. Moreover, students and teachers from different schools were soon competing in designing attractive landscapes, planting shrubs and flowers, introducing novel color schemes, fashioning outdoor sculptures, and otherwise beautifying their schools.

The obvious moral of this final parable applies as well to all the others: planning educational facilities calls for unconventional thinking and great ingenuity, backed up by good pedagogical judgment and competent cost analysis. Planners should devise temporary solutions to meet temporary needs, but even to meet enduring needs, they should seek flexible solutions. For if there is to be a revolution of teaching-learning technologies, as there clearly must be, this will require a kind of architectural flexibility and ingenuity that will not suffocate new educational ideas and practices.

Identifying and Measuring Capital Costs

As noted previously, practical accounting problems arise in distinguishing between capital costs and recurrent costs. Conceptually, the distinction is clear enough. To reiterate, capital costs are associated with durable educational inputs—particularly land and site improvements (e.g., sewer lines), buildings, furniture, and equipment—that give service for more than a single fiscal year. Recurrent costs, by contrast, involve services and supplies that can be consumed within a single year. The practical line of demarcation between capital and recurrent costs must often be drawn arbitrarily, and can create confusion in accounting systems.

By the above definition, books are capital items because they usually last for several years. Thus common practice is to treat the initial bulk purchase of textbooks and library books for a new school or university as a capital outlay. Equally common practice, however, is to treat the purchase of additional books and replacements thereafter as a current expense. The latter violates a theoretical nicety, but in this case no harm is done so long as the same accounting method is used consistently.

The treatment of major repairs and replacements that prolong the life of existing capital items is another problem area. If these irregular and frequently sizable expenditures are not adequately provided for on schedule, which is often what happens when they are treated incorrectly as current costs and thrown into direct competition with teacher costs, the result can be serious physical deterioration of capital, disruption of educational programs, increased inefficiency, higher future costs, and lowered productivity. One way to avert this risk is to set up a special capital reserve account for major repairs and replacements that can be added to annually and drawn upon as needed, independently of the recurrent budget.

Educational systems in developing nations will also be well advised to keep a special foreign currency reserve earmarked for the prompt purchase of replacement parts for imported equipment, as well as a minimal inventory of critical spare parts. Otherwise, each time a machine breaks down, the educational process may be disrupted for many weeks due to the time consuming process of obtaining an official allocation of foreign exchange and of ordering and awaiting delivery of the needed parts.

The following basic concepts will help you unravel confusing accountng records and avoid errors in measuring capital costs.

Capital Stocks Versus Capital Flow

The stock of capital is the inventory of buildings, equipment, and other capital items that exist at a given point in time. It is like a reservoir that can be drawn down (by depreciation) or replenished and enlarged by new inflows. You can measure the value of an educational system's capital stock by depreciating the original cost of each item in the inventory at an appropriate rate, adjusted for major repairs, additions, and replacements made in the interim. Alternatively, you can measure it by estimating the replacement value (what it would cost today to replace the facilities), minus depreciation. Or you can measure it by its estimated market value if the information for making such an estimate is available.

These distinct concepts and measurements—of capital stock at a particular time, of capital inflows over past years, and of new inflows needed in future years—are basic tools for a variety of practical purposes. You will need them to estimate total unit costs per student in different parts of the educational system, to measure the full costs of education to the economy, to compare the relative merits of alternative courses of action, to cost individual projects, to project future capital fund requirements, and to apply cost-benefit tests.

Depreciation and Amortization

In addition to the stock and flow concepts, there is the important concept of spreading the costs of capital items over their useful lifetime in order to allocate a proper share of these costs to each time period and to each group served. This method is essential to determine the total unit cost per student (recurrent cost plus capital cost) and to make cost-benefit assessments, such as rate of return studies.

You can spread capital costs over time by applying an appropriate depreciation charge to each year, with the rate of depreciation varying with the expected useful life of each item; but this is not the whole story. For most purposes, you should add interest costs to depreciation costs, which give you the amortization cost. In the case of an educational facility built with an interest bearing loan, the annual amortization cost equals the portion of the principal paid off each year plus the interest owed (the total of the two is called "debt service").

Even when the budget shows no interest cost, when estimating full capital costs, you must include an imputed interest charge that reflects what the capital would earn in some alternative use in the economy. In this manner, you can arrive at an imputed rent for all capital facilities that you can use to estimate total education costs (or unit cost per student) in any one year or over a period of years. (Of course, in the rare cases where schools actually occupy rented premises, your estimates will include the actual rent instead of an imputed rent.)

Budgetary Costs Versus Full Costs

Our earlier caveats about public and private costs, as well as budgetary costs versus costs to the economy, apply with special force to capital costs. Remember always to ask the operative questions: What kind of costs do I want to measure? And cost to whom? If, for example, you are only concerned at the moment with estimating capital requirements to be met through government budgets, which will often be the case, it is legitimate to ignore private capital outlays and the full costs to the economy, so long as you are aware of these omissions. If, however, your aim is to measure the nation's total capital outlays on education, you must include an estimate for private outlays. Or if you are attempting to assess the full costs to the economy, you must estimate the opportunity costs of all capital used by education, including both the existing stock and any new inflows.

Domestic Versus Foreign Costs

When you are projecting future capital requirements, you must distinguish between those to be met from domestic resources and those that you hope will be financed by foreign resources (see the example of Tanzania in table 4-1). Often, setting a value on foreign supplied facilities in terms of their equivalent domestic costs instead of using the actual cost to the foreign donor or lender is also desirable. This is important, for example, if you are assessing the value of the present capital stock, or if you are estimating what

85

it would cost to replicate with domestic resources a pilot facility supplied from abroad.

The several foregoing distinctions can help you untangle budget forms and accounting records which, from the cost analyst's point of view, frequently "mix apples and bananas." Often, for example, the official education budget includes both debt service on facilities built in the past and capital funds needed to build new facilities. If you include both these figures in an annual time series of capital expenditures, you will be guilty of double counting. Choose whichever best serves your purpose, but never add them together. There are many similar accounting pitfalls that the above concepts can help you avoid.

Constructing a Time Series of Capital Expenditures

One of your first exercises should be to construct an annual time series of capital outlays, running back several years. This will put the past in perspective and shed useful light on the future. You can do this fairly easily. Capital outlays from public funds can usually be extracted without great difficulty from public budget accounts; but to get a full national picture, you will have to include private outlays as well. Obtaining these private figures is generally harder, and you may have to estimate them. You can do this quite simply if you have annual figures on the number of new classrooms or the amount of new space added to various types of private institutions. Apply to these physical quantities the cost factors derived from public construction experience with similar types of facilities in the same period. The resulting estimate will be rough, but it will usually suffice. (Again, remember not to double count public subsidies for the construction of private education facilities.)

We suggest the following guidelines for constructing a time series of capital outlays:

1. Use actual expenditures where possible rather than budgetary allotment figures; they are a much more accurate measure of what actually happened.

2. Separate expenditures on new facilities and equipment from expenditures on major repairs or replacements that simply maintain old facilities.

3. Break down the capital total at least by education levels and, if possible, by categories of institutions (for example, day schools versus residential schools, general secondary schools versus technical schools; rural versus urban schools.

4. Make an annual breakdown by sources of capital funds especially separating funds from domestic and foreign sources, from public versus private domestic sources, and from different levels of government.

5. Once you have put the whole picture together in terms of current prices, translate the series into constant prices, using an educational construction cost index as a price deflator.

These breakdowns will provide a picture not only of the overall trend of capital outlays but, equally important, of any changes in the pattern of allocation within the educational system (which has important implications for the future pattern of recurrent costs), and changes in the pattern of sources of capital funds (which may provide important clues to future financing possibilities).

Do not be surprised if the resulting time series of capital flows shows a very erratic movement of outlays from year to year (in contrast to the much smoother curve of recurrent expenditures that you obtained in the exercise in chapter 5). A variety of factors cause sharp annual fluctuations in capital outlays: discontinuities in the flow of foreign aid, spasmodic decisions to launch major new educational programs, and ups and downs in the economy and in the flow of public revenues.

The wide fluctuations of capital expenditures between 1975 and 1981 as a percentage of total public expenditures on education are illustrated in table 6-1 for a sample of 16 developing countries. Be cautious in making inter-country comparisons from this table because the figures are not strictly comparable due to differences in national accounting practices. It is likely, for example, that some nations reported capital outlays from both domestic and foreign sources, while others included only domestic sources; some countries may have included repairs, replacements, and debt service charges along with expansion of facilities, while others did not.

Table 6-1. Annual Fluctuations of Capital Expenditures as a Percentage of Total Educational Expenditures, 1975-1981

Country	Highest year (percentage)		Lowest year (percentage)	
Algeria	34.9	(1979)	8.0	(1978)
Arab Republic of Egypt	21.4	(1981)	14.0	(1975)
Ethiopia	26.5	(1976)	16.2	(1979)
Madagascar	22.4	(1981)	4.8	(1979)
Morocco	21.4	(1978)	13.8	(1975)
Socialist People's Libyan Arab Jamchiriya	45.5	(1975)	32.0	(1979)
Tunisia	15.4	(1978)	6.2	(1981)
Costa Rica	8.7	(1980)	6.5	(1981)
Nicaragua	12.8	(1980)	1.8	(1979)
Colombia	19.5	(1978)	5.2	(1979)
Peru	5.6	(1980)	3.6	(1975)
India	1.3	(1979)	0.9	(1975)
Malaysia	18.2	(1981)	9.7	(1979)
Pakistan	30.0	(1975)	25.7	(1979)
Saudi Arabia	57.3	(1975)	33.5	(1978)
Thailand	32.0	(1978)	23.0	(1981)

Source: UNESCO 1983, table 4.1.

Determining Future Capital Needs

To project the capital funds required for a new planning period, say, five years, you must begin with an estimate of physical needs. These include
1. necessary repairs and replacements to maintain existing facilities in good condition;
2. modifications and additions to existing facilities and equipment to support qualitative changes in educational processes and programs, such as

the introduction of instructional television, team teaching, or more ample laboratory facilities; and

3. net additions to present capacity needed to accommodate more students, either by enlarging existing institutions on the same site or by building separate, new facilities.

The best way to estimate the first component (repairs and replacements) is on the basis of a full physical survey of all existing facilities, which will give you a schedule of needed repairs and replacements for each institution. Where this is not feasible, the second best method is to survey a representative sample of institutions, classified by age, size, function, type of construction and equipment, and climatic conditions. Then apply the repair and replacement needs derived from this sample to the whole establishment.

If the sampling approach is not feasible, you will have to use a much cruder method based on recent past expenditures for repairs and replacements (adjusted upward if you have reason to believe that there has been considerable deferred maintenance in the past). Even for this crude method, you must secure, if possible, a full list of existing facilities (perhaps from central records of the ministry), classified according to the same characteristics as those suggested above for a sample survey. With the help of an experienced building engineer, you can work out a set of repair and replacement norms to apply to each category. Obviously the older institutions and those made of materials that deteriorate more rapidly, plus those with more complex equipment, such as technical schools, will have the highest repair and replacement requirements. Your total estimate may seem small relative to capital requirements for new construction (if your educational system is expanding rapidly), but the matter nonetheless deserves careful attention, because skimping on maintenance can eventually result in eroding existing capital assets and can prove to be an extremely expensive way to "save" a little money in the short run.

You must estimate the second type of capital requirement (modifications and additions) on an ad hoc basis, program by program. If, for example, a new science program for secondary schools calls for new types of laboratory equipment, you will have to work out the requirements and cost them in terms of a list of needed equipment, the number of schools involved, and a time schedule for procurement and installation. Estimating the capital requirements for installing instructional television is somewhat more complicated, but the basic method is essentially the same. It is more complicated because a greater variety and complexity of equipment is involved (at both the broadcasting and receiving end); because it may be necessary to provide electric power sources to some schools and to modify classroom space for efficient reception; and because repair facilities may also have to be created.[2]

---

[2] Plans for introducing educational broadcasting have often foundered badly on two counts. First, no provision was made for ensuring a reliable repair and maintenance service, with the result that the sending or receiving equipment was out of use much of the time. Second, most of the budget went into the "hardware," with little left to create good quality and effective "software" (program content), leading to disappointing pedagogical results.

The third type of capital requirement (additions) is quantitatively the most important when an educational system is expanding rapidly, and therefore deserves your special attention.

The greatest mistake usually made in projecting the capital requirements for an expansion program is to assume (tacitly) that existing facilities are already being used to capacity, and therefore that the stock of facilities must be expanded by the same percentage as the expected increase in enrollments. This is rarely the case. Even in systems where some classrooms are grossly overcrowded, many others may have undersized classes. Moreover, accommodating more students in existing facilities is often possible by modifying the academic time schedule. Hence we strongly recommend that you conduct a space utilization survey before calculating the need for new facilities and equipment. In short, before scarce resources are committed to building new facilities, you should make every effort to ensure that the best use is being made of the existing ones.

A space utilization survey of secondary schools in several African countries by UNESCO's Regional Educational Building Institute (REBIA) illustrates what such a survey may reveal. The study in Morocco showed that "in almost all the schools surveyed, the available number of spaces is more than that required by a considerable margin . . . in the general classroom category by an average of 17.45 percent, in the science laboratory category by an average of 33.33 percent, and in the special classroom category by an average of 15 percent (REBIA 1969a). A similar survey in Ghana concluded that "in all space categories dealt with, it is apparent that provision has been made for more spaces than what is actually required to meet the needs." The average excess capacity in general classrooms was 28.69 percent, in special purpose classrooms 42.69 percent, and in science laboratories 33.33 percent (REBIA 1969b).

You should interpret space utilization figures cautiously, however, for even the best managed educational system is unlikely to achieve 100 percent utilization. There are a number of reasons: schools in one area may be losing students to another area; new schools are filling up, but are not as yet full; daily absentees leave desks unfilled; and the academic time schedule imposes substantial idle time on all facilities.[3] Even after allowing for such factors, however, there is usually a sizable cushion for improving the use of expensive facilities. By bringing the facts of underutilization to light, cost analysts can encourage decisions in favor of greater efficiency.

Limits exist, of course, as to what systems can achieve without impairing educational effectiveness. Just where these limits are must be determined case by case in each locality, but in making such determinations, it is important that they be based on evidence developed by practical experimentation and observation, not simply on traditional practice and educational mythology.

---

[3]   A useful indicator for diagnostic and planning purposes would be an index of occupied student places. Taken alongside the index of student places, this indicator would provide a running measure of space utilization. Used for planning, it would make allowance for absentees and other factors that cause a normal underutilization of available student places.

Once education officials have made plans for the full and efficient use of existing facilities and established the need for a net increase in facilities, the next problem is to choose the best size and location for the new structures; to decide when to add to existing facilities (which is usually cheaper) and when to create new ones; to strike the right balance between different types of facilities (for example, day schools versus boarding schools); and to plan the optimum use of new facilities, for example, by adopting efficient time schedules, by using technical schools in off-hours for adult training, and other schools for general community purposes. By exploring and costing all such alternatives, you can help blaze a trail toward more and better education for more people at affordable costs.

Estimating the Costs of Capital Expansion

Once you have established the real physical needs for new facilities, the next step is to estimate what it will cost to meet them. Here again, the best methods to use will depend on the particular purpose and circumstances. If you are costing a specific project, such as a new teacher training institution for which specifications have already been drawn, the costing should be much more refined and tailored to the specifications than if you are making an overall estimate of capital fund requirements for a whole five-year national educational plan.

The Role of Physical Norms and Prototypes

Even overall capital requirements estimates must be tied to some sort of physical specifications, otherwise they are meaningless. Such physical specifications in turn must be related to what will go on in and around the new buildings, what educational aims and functions are to be served, what educational process is to be used, and what types of learners are to be served, including how many and for what periods of time. Thus, for example, projecting costs for primary schools obviously involves a very different set of physical norms than costing secondary technical schools or an agricultural college. In short, capital cost estimates must be based either on specific architectural plans or, for more general estimating, on a series of prototypes and norms that fit the variety of physical requirements foreseen in the forthcoming plan period.

The more varied these prototypes are to fit varying categories and circumstances, and the more that future overall enrollment projections can be broken down into these categories, the more accurate the capital cost projections will be. In a typical developing country, having standard cost estimates for at least the number of prototypes shown in table 6-2 is desirable. Obviously, you will have to adapt the classifications shown in the table to the country's educational structure and practices. A British type of system, for example, might classify secondary schools by the number of "streams." Where appropriate, you could add various prototypes of postsecondary institutions, such as teacher training colleges or advanced rural institutes. Universities or other major institutions, however, are likely to require separate, tailor-made estimates, since each one is so individual.

Before discussing how to cost these prototypes, a brief word is in order about new trends in setting physical standards for schools. Traditionally, physical standards for school construction have either been extremely hap-

Table 6.2. Illustration of Standard Cost Prototype

School level and type	Cost per pupil place	Single-shift enrollment capacity	Capital total cost
Primary			
Single-room school (rural)			
2 classrooms (rural)			
3 to 6 classrooms (rural, semirural)			
6 to 12 classrooms (urban)			
Over 12 classrooms (urban)			
Secondary			
6 or less classrooms			
7 to 12 classrooms			
Over 12 classrooms			
Technical schools			
Secondary (residential)			
12 or less classrooms			
Over 12 classrooms			

hazard or excessively rigid. The rigid ones have typically been defined in such terms as the minimum or maximum floor space required per student; the ratio of window space to square feet of working area; minimum-maximum ceiling heights; required number of doors per room; the proportions of classroom space, corridor space, and other types of space; number of toilet stalls and playground area per 100 students, and so on. In the extreme, a single school design has been imposed by the central ministry on every community, whether it fitted local conditions or not.

People are changing their thinking about prototypes these days and moving toward an intermediate between *laissez-faire* and total rigidity. In a number of countries (the United Kingdom is a good example), teams of imaginative architects, educators, engineers, and cost analysts have fashioned new approaches to the more efficient design, construction, and use of educational structures, and to enhancing their aesthetic and psychological features as well. One of the outcomes has been the creation of *performance* or *functional* standards, as distinct from the old-fashioned, rigid *physical* specifications that leave little room for local ingenuity and adaptation (see MacLure 1984 for an account of the United Kingdom's experience). For example, instead of specifying a fixed ratio of window space to floor space, the new norms simply indicate the minimum strength of light required in all working areas, leaving it to the ingenuity of architects and lighting engineers to determine how they can meet this functional norm in a given situation. Similarly, local educators and architects are given latitude (within a prescribed cost ceiling) to make trade-offs between classroom space and other space, such as administrative offices, corridors,

91

cafeterias, auditoriums, that will provide maximum flexibility and educational advantage.

We strongly recommend that educational planners and cost analysts try to keep abreast of new ideas on school buildings through the publications and advice of such organizations as UNESCO's Regional School Building Centers, the Educational Facilities Laboratory of the Academy for Educational Development in New York, the World Bank's Department of Education and Training, and ministries of education in such countries as France, Spain, and the United Kingdom that have been fostering new approaches to school construction.

Costing Project Designs and Prototypes

Once an architect has drawn up the plans for a particular facility, professional cost engineers usually develop a detailed cost estimate for the project. Prior to that stage, general educational cost analysts (with whatever help they can get from construction experts) must work out rougher cost estimates. For the most part, this means arriving at the best possible "standard costs" for the various prototypes referred to above, along with certain "adjustment factors" that you can apply to the nationwide standard costs to allow for regional cost variations, interim price changes, or any other important differentials, for example, the difference in construction costs between urban and rural areas may be considerable. For some purposes, however, such as costing innovations and qualitative changes in existing facilities, you must use other methods.

By and large, the best unit to express the costs of different prototypes is the *capital cost per student place*. Once you have determined this figure, you can apply it to the number of additional students that must be provided for in each category (for example, rural primary students, secondary boarding students) to determine the overall capital funding required for each category.

The advantage of using the cost per student place (as against the cost per classroom) is that it averages out differences in the sizes of classes and classrooms in different schools, as well as variations in the ratio of classroom space to other space. For the same reason, cost per student place makes the best costing unit for setting cost limits and enforcing them, without tying the hands of architects and local school authorities.

When it comes to costing the installation of a television system, however, the number of classrooms and the cost per classroom (rather than the number of student places) is a better unit to use for costing the television sets, whereas the number of school broadcast hours required to cover desired portions of the curriculum is the best unit to determine the size and cost of the broadcasting facilities needed.

The costing of furniture and equipment, whether for prototypes or specific projects, calls for a list of items needed to fit the requirements of a given size and type of facility. You should cost the equipment and furniture bill at the best prices available on items meeting minimum standards.

The best way to establish standard costs for prototypes is on the basis of recent actual costs for a sample of projects as representative as possible of those to be built in the future. (If future structures are to differ drastically from previous ones, you may require a different method of costing. If possible, the sample for each prototype should include no fewer than six cases to average out wide variations, particularly in land, site preparation, and site

utility costs (which usually vary much more from project to project than construction and equipment costs). Analyze the sample cases with the following minimum cost breakdown:
- land acquisition (total area and per square foot)
- site clearance and improvement
- installation of site utilities and service
- construction of structures
- equipment and furnishing
- architectural and other fees.

You can next analyze and aggregate the cost data from the same cases for each prototype and express it in various useful ways, as illustrated in table 6-3. Take note that the projects in the sample will probably have been built at different times; hence, you will need an educational construction price index to translate them into comparable current and prospective prices before you average them and enter them on a summary table.

Analysis of the various samples should also give you a standard set of geographic differentials in land and construction costs that you can use to calculate deviations from the nationwide standard costs when costing re gional components of overall national construction plans. You can use the construction price index to adjust for cost increases that have occurred since the base date for the standard costs, and to project future increases.

Table 6-3. Examples of Standard Characteristics and Costs of a Prototype Urban Primary School

---

1. Typical number of student places   _____
2. Cost per student place $_____
3. Land area (mean average)   _____sq. ft.
4. Total building area (mean average)   _____sq. ft.
5. Costs (actual)
    - a. Land and site survey $_____
    - b. Site improvement and utilities $_____
    - c. Construction materials $_____
    - d. Construction labor $_____
    - e. Construction cost per square foot $_____
    - f. Equipment, furniture, etc. $_____
    - g. Architects' and other fees $_____
    - h. Total $_____
6. Costs (percentage breakdown)
    - a. Construction   _____%
    - b. Architects' and other fees:
      _____% of (a)   _____%
    - c. Equipment and furniture   _____%
    - d. Land and site survey   _____%
    - e. Site improvement and utilities   _____%
    - f. Total   100%

You can use the standard costs and price adjustment factors described above not only for costing an overall national school expansion plan, region by region and level by level, but also for making initial rough cost estimates for more limited subsystems, even individual projects. Table 6-4 shows a worksheet for calculating the costs of a subsystem.

Methods similar to those outlined above were used in Thailand to estimate the costs of building three similar vocational schools, each to accommodate 450 students, in three different locations. Although this was done in the mid1960s and the specific cost figures are now obsolete, the results shown in table 6-5 still serve to illustrate our point. You will see that the construction and equipment costs, based on standard costs, are very similar for all three schools, except that the construction costs of school 2 ran 10 percent higher than the other two because of regional cost differences. The land, site improvement, and utilities costs, however, varied widely. You should always look at the latter three items in combination. Often a "bargain" on the land cost can be much more than offset by high sit improvement and utility costs. In the Thai case, school 3 had land costs of only 700,000 bahts compared to 2,000,000 bahts for school 2, yet their combined land, site improvement, and utility costs were roughly equal (2,540,000 bahts versus 2,600,000 bahts).

Table 6-4. Summary Worksheet for Calculating Capital Costs of Expanding an Educational Subsystem

A. Category of facility_____

B. Typical enrollment capacity _____

C. Breakdown of costs
   1. Standard cost of structure
   2. Site improvement and utility services
      _____ %
   3. Total (1 + 2)   _____
   4. Adjustment of (3) for interim cost increases
      _____ %   _____
 * 5. Adjustment of (4) for regional cost
      differences _____ %   _____
 * 6. Architect's and site supervision fees
      _____ %   _____
 * 7. Cost of land and site survey
      _____ %   _____
   8. Standard cost of furniture & equipment   _____
   9. Adjustment of (8) for interim price increases
      _____ %   _____
  10. Adjustment of (9) for regional price
      differences _____ %   _____
  11. Total cost per institution (5+6+7+10)   _____
  12. Total cost of projected program
      _____ %   _____

* Components of total cost (11).

Table 6-5. Thailand: Estimates of Capital Costs of Three Similar Vocational Schools, 1965

Item	School 1 (bahts)	% of total cost	School 2 (bahts)	% of total cost	School 3 (bahts)	% of total cost
Construction costs						
1. Space for administration, classrooms, and library	1,710,000	17.1	1,881,000	14.8	1,710,000	15.1
2. Workshop	2,760,000	27.5	3,036,000	23.9	2,280,000	20.2
3. Cafeteria	550,000	5.5	605,000	4.8	550,000	4.9
4. Dormitories	1,704,000	17.0	1,874,000	14.8	1,704,000	15.1
5. Staff Housing	700,000	7.0	770,000	6.1	700,000	6.2
6. Sanitation services	1,305,000	13.0	1,435,000	11.3	1,305,000	11.6
Total	8,729,000	87.0	9,601,000	75.6	8,249,000	73.1
Construction cost per place	19,398		21,337		18,331	
Other costs						
1. Site improvements	400,000	4.0	400,000	3.1	1,240,000	11.0
2. Utilities	400,000	4.0	200,000	1.6	600,000	5.3
3. Equipment	500,000	5.0	500,000	3.9	500,000	4.4
4. Land	--		2,000,000	15.7	700,000	6.2
Total	1,300,000	13.0	3,100,000	24.4	3,040,000	26.9
Grand Total	10,029,000	100.0	12,701,000	100.0	11,289,000	100.0
Total cost per place	22,287		28,226		25,088	

* Totals do not add up due to rounding.

International Norms and Comparisons

Unfortunately, we can offer no tidy international norms for educational capital costs or any standard ratios between the major components of such costs that individual nations could use to assess their own past performance and future costs. This is because of the substantial variations in cost conditions even within the same nation; the variations are much greater between nations. In a poor nation, for example, construction labor may be relatively cheap compared to the costs of materials and equipment (especially if much of the latter must be imported), whereas in a rich country quite the reverse may be true. Similarly, the costs of land and materials may be much cheaper relative to labor in one developing country than another because it has a lower population/land ratio and a more abundant supply of wood, clay, and other raw materials to use in construction. Thus, each country must establish its own appropriate costing norms.

This is not to say, however, that countries cannot profit greatly from one another's experience in educational construction and costing. Quite the contrary is true.

7. Concluding Remarks

We conclude this book with a few general remarks about putting cost analysis into practice. Previous chapters demonstrated a variety of ways in which educational administrators can use cost analysis to increase the efficiency and effectiveness of any educational process and to help attack the formidable problems that have besieged educational systems throughout the world in recent years. However, these beneficial achievements do not happen automatically, regardless of how sound the cost analysis may be. The practical contributions of cost analysis are strongly conditioned—and sometimes defeated—by the type of planning, decision-making process, and management style to which the cost analysis is tied.

Despite the many useful efforts that have been made over the years to improve educational planning, policymaking, and management, educational administrators agree that further major improvements are still needed. For example, educational planning as actually practiced in many countries is frequently criticized for concentrating too narrowly on quantitative expansion to the neglect of needed qualitative changes and improvements; for being too centralized and "top-down" and ignoring important variations in environmental conditions and the learning needs of different localities; and for failing to pay sufficient attention to the practical requirements for translating a written plan into actions.

Similarly, educational policymaking and decision making are criticized for being too fragmented, episodic, and incoherent; for often ignoring the results of cost analysis and the work of planners; and for being unduly influenced and distorted by special interest groups and by the whims and self-interest of politicians. By the same token, prevailing modes of educational administration also suffer from serious shortcomings.

Meanwhile, troubled educational authorities all over the world are eagerly seeking practical answers to such perplexing questions as the following:

• What can we do to halt and reverse the deterioration of educational quality and relevance?

• How can we make our education more compatible with the world of work and with the broad and changing needs of individual and national development.

• What are the most effective and affordable means for reducing the serious educational disparities and inequalities that are handicapping various disadvantaged groups, impeding rural development, and exacerbating our

• What can we do to overcome the present critical shortage of educational resources and the worsening cost-finance squeeze on our educational system that hinder our ability to cope effectively with the above problems?

There are, of course, no easy answers to these questions, much less any magic solutions to fit all countries. Each country must devise its own set of policies and actions to fit its own particular circumstances and capabilities. In so doing, however, all countries can profit from some important lessons of experience that are relevant to many countries throughout the world. Since our proposal for action is based on these lessons, we shall examine a few of the most important ones.

Lessons of Experience

Lesson 1 is that educational systems everywhere must change continuously to adapt to the major changes taking place in their economic, technological, social, cultural, and political environment. They must also make changes so as to serve the more diverse learning needs and learning styles of their greatly enlarged and more diversified student clientele, as well as to achieve a more efficient and effective use of their limited available resources.

This compelling need for major educational changes and innovations calls for a different kind of educational planning. Most countries retained the largely quantitative kind of planning associated with the widely adopted strategy of linear expansion of inherited educational systems. This latter strategy has been a major contributor to the growing maladjustment between educational systems and the rapidly changing world all around them.

Lesson 2 is that a fragmented, piecemeal approach to these needed changes is insufficient. To cope effectively with today's critical educational issues requires a much more comprehensive, dynamic, and integrated "package approach" that views the entire educational system *as* a system. It also requires major attention to possible alternative ways to achieve desired educational results that could be more appropriate and more cost-effective than traditional ways.

Lesson 3 is that in the future, educational systems will require a much more flexible and broadly based system of management, in contrast to the highly centralized and bureaucratized management system that exists in most countries today. It must be a more open system of management that encourages participation by interested and responsible people at all levels, and that can respond to significant differences in local conditions and learning needs. For decisions and actions at every level to be well informed, and for the system's performance to be steadily monitored and evaluated, it must have a strengthened information system and analytical capacity, and improved provision for two-way communication between all parts and levels of the system and with the general public. Cost analysis is an essential building block leading to such a strengthened information system. The appalling shortage of educational data and of evaluation in most countries today obliges their educational managers to move into the future half blind.

Lesson 4 is that well-conceived interdisciplinary research can be a powerful instrument for guiding needed educational change and for improving the performance of any educational system or activity. To be really useful, however, such research must differ greatly from the usual activities of educational researchers. Needless to say, in this context, it should be strongly based on sound data on costs of education and on true educational inputs and outcomes. The research designs must be formulated and carried out in close concert with educational practitioners. It must be directed at questions

97

and problems of genuine concern to these users of research, and the findings communicated to them in clear, comprehensible, jargon-free language. Unfortunately, much educational research in the past has failed to meet these criteria and consequently contributed little or nothing to educational improvement.

The Need for A Critical Assessment of Education

We suggest, in concluding this book, that cost analysis should become part of a major assessment of countries' education systems and ways in which they may accomplish national objectives for greater learning within the very limited funds available for education. We suggest that countries should undertake a critical assessment of their education situation and of recent trends and projections.

In our opinion, although the assessment should focus initially on the formal education system, it should nevertheless keep in view important complementary learning activities outside the formal system. Experience indicates to us that, in view of the cost constraints on formal education, non-formal education may be the only avenue through which countries can serve the steadily evolving learning needs of an entire population, including not only school-age children but also pre-schoolers, out-of-school youth, and adults.

Admittedly a nationwide assessment is an ambitious undertaking, but it would be more than justified by the great importance of the subject and by the massive public and private resources being invested in education. Moreover, it would provide a rare opportunity to involve a wide range of people, both inside and outside the educational system, in examining the system's internal affairs and its relation to national needs and resources. Such involvement could stimulate their interest in education, deepen their understanding of why major changes are needed, sensitize them to the practical resource limitations, give rise to a variety of potentially useful ideas, and ultimately help to develop a broad consensus in support of the actions finally decided upon.

Once the assessment has identified the principal strengths and shortcomings in the current educational situation and the kinds of future needs to be met, the next step is to examine and weigh the relative feasibility and cost-effectiveness of alternative ways to strengthen the system's performance. This analytical process, in which cost analysis would play an important role, leads to the making of choices and decisions that will lead to an education system that is efficient and effective in achieving the country's learning objectives. We feel that better information, including information on educational costs, can have a powerful positive effect on education and on economic and social development.

References

Coombs, Philip H. 1985. *The World Crisis in Education: The View From the Eighties*. New York: Oxford University Press. (See selected reading list for description.)

Coombs, Philip H., and Jacques Hallak. 1972. *Managing Educational Costs*. London: Oxford University Press.

Levin, H. M. 1983. *Cost-Effectiveness: A Primer*. Beverley Hills, CA: Sage Publications.

Jamison, D. T., and E. G. McAnany. 1978. *Radio for Education and Development*. Beverley Hills, CA: Sage Publications.

Maclure, Stuart. 1984. *Educational Development and School Building: Aspects of Public Policy 1945-73*. London: Longman.

Oliveira, J. G., and F. Orivel. 1978. *Analyse socio-economique de trois systemes d'enseignement à distance au Bresil*. Washington, D.C.: The World Bank.

Psacharopoulos, George, and Maureen Woodhall. 1985. *Education for Development: An Analysis of Investment Choices*. New York: Oxford University Press for the World Bank. Chapter 3. (See selected reading list for description.)

Radi, M. 1982. *Study of Operating Costs of Secondary Schools in Morocco*. IIEP files.

REBIA. 1969a. *Space Utilization Survey of Secondary Schools—Morocco*. Khartoum: REBIA.

REBIA. 1969b. *Space Utilization Survey of Secondary Schools—Ghana*. Khartoum: REBIA.

UNESCO. 1977, 1980, 1982. *The Economics of New Educational Media*. 3 vols. Paris: UNESCO.

UNESCO. 1983. *Statistical Yearbook*.

UNESCO. 1984. *The Worldwide Evolution of Student Wastage at the Primary Level Between 1970 and 1980*. Paris: UNESCO.

World Bank. 1980. *World Development Report*. Washington, D.C.: The World Bank.

Selected Reading List

The titles listed below are only a small sample of the rapidly growing body of useful literature (in English) bearing on educational costs and finance. We selected these particular items not only for their inherent interest, but to illustrate the diversity of available materials in this field. Several contain lengthy bibliographies of other useful publications.

Ahmed, M. 1975. *The Economics of Nonformal Education; Resources, Costs and Benefits*. New York: Praeger Publishers.
A down to earth discussion of ways to view the costs and effectiveness of nonformal education, illustrated with examples from case studies by the International Council for Educational Development.

Charfoor, A. 1982. *The Effects of New Trends in Educational Financing on the Plan Objectives: Equity, Quality and Efficiency*. An Occasional Paper of UNESCO's Regional Office. Bangkok: UNESCO.
An interesting case study of changes in Pakistan's historical pattern of educational financing, and the situation under the fifth Five-Year Plan (1978-1983). The report also discusses the financial implications of universal primary education, and of the optimal resource allocation by education levels.

Cohn, E. 1979. *The Economics of Education*. Cambridge, MA: Ballinger Publishing Co.
This updated version of an earlier book provides a broad survey of different aspects of the economics of education and a "literature guide" of over 2,000 titles.

Coombs, P. H. 1985. *The World Crisis in Education: The View from the Eighties*. New York: Oxford University Press.
This sequel to the author's earlier book on this subject (1968) shows how the worldwide educational crisis has steadily worsened since the early 1970s and is likely to plague all countries for years to come. Individual chapters, based on evidence from many sources, probe into various major issues that cut across both developing and industrialized countries, such as the explosive growth of learning needs, the deterioration of educational quality and relevance, rising youth unemployment, gross educational inequalities, the weakening of international education cooperation, and the growing educational cost-finance squeeze that complicates all the other issues. The author concludes that the only way to bring the crisis under control is by major changes in educational policies and practices. The book's many charts and tables make it a useful reference source.

Educational Testing Service, International Office. 1979. *A Manual for the Analysis of Cost and Outcomes in Non-Formal Education.* Princeton: Educational Testing Service.
A valuable tool kit for practitioners responsible for planning, administering, and evaluating nonformal educational activities in developing countries. Includes many illustrations.

Eicher, J. C. 1984. *Educational Costing and Financing in Developing Countries.* World Bank Staff Working Papers, No. 655. Washington, DC: The World Bank.
This paper focuses primarily on the Francophone countries of West Africa, but is useful to cost analysts in all countries. It includes a penetrating critique of the shortcomings of available international data on educational costs. Beyond this, it provides a crisp analysis of possible ways for a developing country to improve and enlarge its educational services within the confines of a tight public education budget, especially by increasing educational efficiency and by tapping supplemental sources of revenue, particularly from the private sector.

Fielden, J, and R. R. Pearson. 1978. *The Cost of Learning with Computers.* London: Centre for Educational Technology.
A useful book, based on British experience, for anyone contemplating the use of computer assisted learning. Though its cost data are somewhat outdated, it evaluation concepts and methods are still valid and useful.

Fredericksen, B. 1983. *Statistics on Education in Developing Countries: An Introduction to their Collection and Analysis.* Paris: Office of Statistics, UNESCO.
This document discusses purposes, principles, and procedures for collection of education statistics, presents an inventory of the type of statistics needed for planning purposes, and reviews practical problems commonly experienced in developing countries in this area. One section (pp. 44-48) deals with education finance statistics. The author is uniquely qualified on this subject by his extensive experience with assisting various developing countries to improve their education statistics.

Inter-American Development Bank. 1979. *The Financing of Education in Latin America.* Washington, DC: Inter-American Development Bank.
This is a report of a seminar on educational financial prospects and policies in Latin America, held in Mexico City in late 1978, and cosponsored by the Mexican government and Inter-American Development Bank. The seminar focused on two broad topics: (1) the relationship between educational expansion, the costs and finances involved, and the impact on socioeconomic development, viewed in the context of each country's historical experience; and (2) the desirability of shifting the emphasis of educational policies and priorities from high unit cost secondary and postsecondary levels to the low unit cost elementary level to improve the poor social and economic status of marginalized low-income families. Participants also considered possible forms of vocational and technical training that might be financed outside the public education budget.

101

International Development Research Center. 1983. *Financing Educational Development*. Ottawa: International Development Research Center.

In May 1982, representatives of over two dozen donor agencies met in Canada with policymakers from developing countries and educational researchers. The meeting was convened to examine the present state of educational costs and finance around the world, the prospects for increasing educational investments in light of increasing financial constraints on developing countries and donor agencies, and possible ways to improve future prospects. This report summarizes the highlights of the discussions and includes several technical papers prepared for the meeting.

Jamison, D. T. 1979. *Cost Factors in Planning Educational Technology Systems*. Fundamental of Educational Planning, No. 24. Paris: UNESCO/IIEP.

An important booklet for anyone contemplating the use of new educational media, particularly radio or television. Based on evaluation studies in many countries, it stresses the major influence of audience size on cost per student hour, and the crucial importance of careful planning and advance preparation.

Lange, R. S. 1983. *Factors Influencing Current Costs of Secondary Education in the Gyo State of Nigeria*. An IIEP research report. Paris: UNESCO/IIEP.

A good demonstration of micro-cost analysis aimed at discovering specific causes of wide variations between the per student cost of 60 secondary schools.

Layne, A. 1985. *"Government Revenue and Expenditure on Education in Barbados."* International Journal of Educational Development. Vol. 5, No. 2.

This article examines the current financial squeeze on education in this former British colony in the context of current economic conditions and government revenues. Especially interesting is its examination of the recently adopted policy measures designed to slow the rate of increase in educational costs.

Levin, H. M. 1983. *Cost Effectiveness-A Primer. Vol. 4 of New Perspectives in Evaluation*. Beverley Hills, CA: Sage Publications.

A clear and useful treatment of concepts and methods for assessing the likely cost-effectiveness of various types of educational innovations prior to adopting them. Includes specific illustrations based on U.S. experience, but relevant for other countries.

Meesook, O. A. 1984. *Financing and Equity in the Social Sectors in Indonesia: Some Policy Options*. World Bank Staff Working Papers, No. 703. Washington, DC: The World Bank.

This is one of several recent World Bank studies that seek to determine the feasibility and equity of shifting more of the costs of education from the public to the private sector. The conclusion reached in the case of Indonesia (and in a number of other World Bank country studies), is that government subsidies for education are skewed toward the rich, especially in higher education, and that a policy of shifting more of the cost burden to the private sector would be both feasible and desirable in terms of increasing total educational resources and reducing educational inequities.

OECD Center for Educational Research and Innovation. 1979. *Educational Financing and Policy Goals for Primary Schools*. Paris: OECD.
These reports (a general report and three volumes of country reports) summarize the results of a two-year study of educational finance. The main focus is on evaluating various financial mechanisms as policy instruments, for instance, for promoting greater equality of educational opportunity, delegating management responsibility, or preserving choice of schooling.

Oliveira, J. B., and F. Orivel. 1982. "A Socioeconomic Analysis of Three Distance Education Systems in Brazil." *In I. Perreton (ed.) Alternative Routes to Formal Education* . Baltimore, MD: Johns Hopkins University Press for the World Bank.
This is another useful study for those interested in the techniques of evaluating the actual or potential cost-effectiveness of distance learning systems.

Psacharopoulos, G., and W. Loxley. 1985. *Diversified Secondary Education and Development*. Baltimore, MD: Johns Hopkins University Press.
During the past decade, many developing countries have sought to improve young people's employment prospects by adding prevocational studies in their academic secondary schools, often with assistance from the World Bank. This comparative study of Colombia and Tanzania is the first systematic attempt to assess the costs and outcomes of such programs and their contribution to national economic development. Officials of any country involved in or contemplating such diversified secondary education will be well-advised to examine the findings of this unique study.

Psacharopoulos, G., and M. Woodhall. 1985. *Education for Development: An Analysis of Investment Choices*. New York: Oxford University Press, A World Bank Publication.
This comprehensive and readable book on the economics of education reflects the lessons learned from the World Bank's extensive activities and studies in the field of educational development and economic growth over the last twenty-five years. It covers such topics as criteria for educational investment, cost-benefit analysis, manpower forecasting, private demand for education, internal efficiency and educational quality, equity considerations, and the intersectoral approach to alleviating poverty. Not surprisingly, the book's major emphasis is on the economic benefits of education (as distinct from its social, psychological, and cultural benefits). It also relies almost exclusively on purely quantitative data and analysis, to the exclusion of important qualitative factors that many observers consider vital. Nevertheless, allowing for these idiosyncracies, the book does what it sets out to do very well.

Psacharopoulos, G., J-P. Tan, and E. Jimenez. 1986. *Financing Education in Developing Countries: An Exploration of Policy Options*.

Washington, DC: The World Bank.
This policy-oriented work argues that education systems must improve their efficiency in times of budgetary austerity. The heavy subsidization of education, especially higher education, which has been traditional policy since most cour*ries gained independence, is no longer appropriate. The book examines three policy options that could improve the balance between resources for education and expenditures: (1) cost recover (i.e., fees) for higher education and reallocation of government spending toward primary education, which has the highest social return; (2) developing student credit arrangements and selective scholarships; and (3) decentralizing the management of education of public education and encouraging development of private and community-supported schools. These policies are examined, using extensive empirical data, and recognizing that their implementation would be difficult in some countries, and not necessarily suitable for all. Still, the authors argue, they would tend to resolve the resource crisis and improve the efficiency and equity of education systems.

Schiefelbein, E. 1983. *Educational Financing in Developing Countries—Research Findings and Contemporary Issues*. Ottawa: International Development Research Center.
This report is based on an extraordinarily comprehensive survey of existing research in this field and will be of particular interest to researchers. It classifies various key issues concerning educational finance, summarizes research conclusions bearing on these issues, and identifies many unsettled questions and research gaps that merit further attention.

Schiefelbein, E., J. Farrel, and M. Speulveda-Stuardo. 1983. *The Influence of School Resources in Chile: Their Effect on Educational Achievement and Occupational Attainment*. World Bank Staff Working Papers, No. 530. Washington, DC: The World Bank.
This paper examines the potential impact of investments in school resources, such as textbooks and other teaching aids, school facilities, and teacher training and retraining. The findings suggest three conclusions: (1) investments in school quality are likely to have a substantial impact on students' success both in school and in the labor market; (2) if they are to have significant impact on students from lower socioeconomic strata, school quality improvements must start early and be accompanied by attention to out-of-school problems, such as malnutrition; (3) the impact of such investments will be increased if they are preceded by studies of current attitudes toward the utilization of school resources, particularly among teachers.

Tan, Jee-Peng. 1985. "The Private Direct Cost of Secondary Schooling in Tanzania." *International Journal of Educational Development*. Vol. 5, No. 1.
This is another of the recent studies on whether fees should be introduced in public educational institutions, in this case, public secondary education in Tanzania. The author cautiously concludes that a possible implication of his research findings is that such user charges could potentially play an important role in mobilizing private household resources for more secondary education, but he cautions that additional research is required to confirm this possibility.

Taylor, D.C. 1983. "The Cost-Effectiveness of Teacher Upgrading by Distance Teaching in Southern Africa." *International Journal of Educational Development*. Vol. 3, No. 1.
Taylor examined several studies of the cost-effectiveness of alternative approaches to upgrading unqualified teachers in Southern Africa. He concludes from these studies that distance teaching programs can be effective and less costly than conventional face-to-face teaching, provided the audience is large enough to achieve substantial economies of scale, and especially if comparative opportunity costs are weighed.

UNESCO. 1977, 1980, 1982. *The Economics of New Educational Media*. 3 volumes. Paris: UNESCO.
These volumes are a rich source of information about methods of evaluating new media projects, and what has been learned thus far about their cost-effectiveness compared to conventional teaching methods. The volumes include a broad review of existing research findings and a variety of interesting case studies, as well as useful analytical concepts and methodologies. Perhaps most important for practicing planners and policymakers are the sober words of caution against underestimating the costs of superimposing the new media on conventional teaching arrangements, and against excessive expectations of the resulting increases in student learning achievements.

UNESCO. 1983. *Training Materials in Educational Planning, Administration and Facilities*. Paris: Division of Education and Planning, UNESCO.
This set of ten training packages is designed to facilitate self-instruction by ministry of education personnel and other interested parties, and for use in national training institutions. It includes sections on cost analysis.